RIPPLES *of* STILLNESS

Simon Peter Moxham

First published in Perth, Western Australia by

E-Touch Communication
www.etherealtouch.com.au
info@etherealtouch.com.au

Ethereal Touch

Copyright © Simon Peter Moxham

All rights reserved, including the right to reproduce this book or portions without the prior written permission of the publisher, except the use of brief quotation.

Cover design and Formatting by:

Graphic Elements
Western Australia
www.graphicelements.com.au

ISBN: 987-0-9945784-0-2

First printed and published in Australia in 2016

First Edition

RIPPLES *of* STILLNESS

Ripples *of* Stillness

For Joy

And all those who have felt her gentle touch

PREFACE

The Doorway

'This is a story about waking up to your highest reality. This is a conversation about finding the light in your eyes.'

The opposite was too terrible to think about.

I wrote this book over a five-month period of my life. I started writing because the opposite was too terrible to think about. You're about to read a daily account of something I went through that changed everything.

It started as a normal story, but quickly became something much bigger. This is a story about waking up to your highest reality. This is a conversation about finding the light in your eyes.

I do not say that after embarking on a pilgrimage where I found extraordinary insight. This story is not about finding a great mentor in the hills of India. I do not come to you after conquering a huge physical feat, or facing some kind of insurmountable demon. This is not a story about surviving against all the odds. I was woken from my slumber in a much simpler way.

That's not to dismiss the experience of others. Stories about great life-changing events have their place, and I'm not here to minimise that. However, my experience tells me that often it is the everyday issues that bring us down. The challenges we face are in the bills we pay. Quite often, our battles are found in the arguments we have with the people we love the most. Sometimes our greatest disappointments come from what we're waiting for rather than what we've faced.

Let me assure you, this is a story about the nuance of life.

Before I started writing I was quietly content going about my life. I was busy paying the bills and looking after my home. My free time was spent with family. I enjoyed playing sport and hanging out with friends. So much of my time was spent relaxing in front of the TV or wandering around different shops. I saw myself as no different to anyone else. I was happy being the guy next door.

I'm a family man who takes the responsibility of being a father very seriously. I have two beautiful teenage daughters. As you are about to find out, in a lot of ways, Jessica and Haylie are my purpose.

Providing for my family is important. I've always worked full-time. I believe a person should earn their place in life. I was devoted to my career as a Child Protection Officer. I worked for the Government of Western Australia, looking after at-risk children in the care of the State. I deliberately studied and went after that job because I wanted to serve. I believe in the virtues of civic duty. Serving the community offered me purpose and fulfilment.

I allowed my job to be a central focus of my life.

I was convinced that if my family was travelling along nicely, and my professional life was thriving, everything would be fine. I found comfort in the routine of life. I had settled into the status quo of that. My task was to minimise the sick days and fortify my nine-to-five.

In many ways, you are reading these words because my career ended abruptly. It wasn't until I left work that I started to change everything. It wasn't until I stopped identifying with my job that I found a new beginning. The reason I walked away from my career is really quite interesting.

Her name is Astrid.

I was in love with her more than the sun shines upon the earth. Just before the beginning of August 2012 our relationship ended. That was my rock bottom. Losing Astrid was when the music stopped.

And that's where my story begins.

Everything I had came crashing in around me. Astrid and I broke down after the pressures from my job buckled our relationship. I was so focused on the success of my career, I didn't notice I was losing her. It was a subtle thing that I'm only able to talk about on reflection.

Astrid and I did not have any massive arguments during our relationship. Our demise did not come from overt aggression, or a shared hatred for each other. It was a slow burn. It was a piece-by-piece type of thing. The breakdown of our relationship was a question of quiet apathy. It came about through not paying attention to each other.

I have experienced plenty of relationship breakups, but losing Astrid was the most heart-wrenching experience I've had. It was the catalyst to waking up to my place in life. It wasn't until I lost my job, and my relationship with Astrid fell apart, that I hit rock bottom. Once I experienced that sort of uncertainty, I felt compelled to square off with myself. I accidentally, but intentionally, confronted my own behaviour. I brought about a change that I will never be able to turn my back on. And even if I could, I would choose not to.

What you are about to read was created after five months of unrelenting self-reflection. My motivation did not come from wanting to write a book or share my experience. I am here for a much simpler reason. I was fed up with hopes and dreams. I started writing about my experience because simply wishing my life would finally make sense wasn't working. Having hopes and dreams without acting on them was keeping my life small.

I wrote this manuscript because I was sick and tired of my own DNA. I was fed up with the routine of life. Initially, the act of writing every day was about doing something different. In my wildest dreams, I couldn't have imagined what was to come. Not in a million years would I have predicted the ripple effect of this thing.

The dialogue kicks off on the 1st of August 2012. It was a Wednesday. Four days earlier, Astrid moved out of our family home after we argued about the pressures I faced at work.

As I sit here now, it's the 20th of May 2016. Almost fours years have passed since I started writing this book. I have rewritten the manuscript three times. I have tweaked it more times than I can count. However, it was extremely important to me that the chronology remained authentic. What I have written actually happened. It just took me four shots at it, and countless little alterations, to settle on the finished product.

I understand that it's not necessarily common for an author to explain his or her work practices in such detail. I only bring it up because what you are about to read is a process of evolution. The act of writing every day is actually part of the story. One of the strengths of the dialogue comes from the growth of what is written.

On reflection, I understand that it starts from a humble place and evolves into the reason I'm sharing it. I'm mindful that the dialogue kicks off from a slightly overcast point of view. I considered changing the start of my reflections so it offered more punch for the reader. But ultimately, I decided not to tamper with the authenticity of what took place.

As I communicate in the first person, I invite you to hear your own voice. Particularly early when I am referring to the pressures I faced. What is true for each of us sits beneath the pressures we face. I did not change the start of the dialogue because I hope you find yourself in what was written.

You are about to see that things became very interesting rather quickly.

I started writing out of desperation. I remember opening my laptop in the middle of the night because I didn't know what else to do. The deprivation I felt was taking hold and I simply acted on instinct. What I have come to realise since, is that the lines of this story did not come from a place of deprivation. Quite the opposite is true. In many respects, I just got out of the way and played witness to what unfolded.

You are reading these words for the same reason I write them. We were meant to share this experience. Understanding that we were meant to find ourselves, in the words before us, brings me great comfort. It is precisely why I offer you this story.

It starts from a humble place. Where it takes you rests in your eyes. This is how we find out what happens next.

PROLOGUE

A Blank Canvas

'It will be your insights that bring this story alive. The depths of those insights will be a result of your creation.'

Prologue

You are precisely where you should be, doing exactly what you are meant to.

I don't just say that because you find yourself reading these words. You are always precisely where you should be. What you've been through accounts for where you are. You are, we all are, but a sum total of where we have come from.

If you are taking the time to read these words you deserve an explanation.

I did not set out to write a book for others. As I've mentioned several times in the dialogue you are about to read, I started writing as a way to pay attention to what I was going through. Initially, it was a simple conversation with myself. I opened the dialogue with no intention of addressing an audience. Consequently, I held nothing back. I wrote as if I was the reader.

What you are about to read happened as I wrote it. Not only is it based on a true story, the chronology is genuine. It's a true account of what took place, written as it was happening. I have not created elaborate examples to emphasise anything. And I do not lead with ambiguous metaphors.

What we will share together is not just my story.

As I just mentioned, when I communicate in the first person I invite you to hear your own voice. The fact that I did not set out to share this material, means I do not have any instructions for you. I have not mapped out any guidelines for success. Nor is there any homework or commitments that will fortify this dialogue. I am simply sharing my story with you. If doing so holds any real potency, it will be because it's about all of us. The strength of the dialogue comes from the things that connect us.

I hope that you're able to look beyond the words you read and see your own reflection. I hope through sharing my story, you find the clarity of yours. As you move through this book, I invite you to wake up to your insights for life. The significance of what we are about to share will not come from my experience but yours. It will be your insights that bring this story alive. The depths of those insights will be a result of your creation, not mine.

However, I have faith this dialogue will spark your instincts. Let there be no other reason you find yourself here in this moment reading these words.

For it is certain, there is no other reason I find myself here in this moment writing them.

This dialogue is an appropriate example of a very old, and somewhat overused saying:

> *'When the student is ready the master will appear'*

I've heard that adage so many times. But I never fully understood it until now. That's not to say that you are the student and I am the master. I am no different to you; you are no different to me. Being ready to learn from 'the master' comes from waking up to your true nature. It comes from understanding the source of your insights.

The evolution of this manuscript is an example of how to find the master for your life within. It was through a process of unrelenting self-reflection that I realised the potential for my life has always been there. I came to understand that the source of my highest reality is a process of creation.

That's an unchangeable fact, and the same indelible truth sits within your heart. When it comes to finding 'the master' of your life, you are the teacher and the student. It is not a question of being in the right place at the right time. Waking up to the insights for your life has nothing to do with luck. Life is a process of creation. The potential for it is found within.

I invite you to come with me now as we create a new beginning together. Let it start with this simple understanding. You are precisely where you should be, doing exactly what you are meant to. The lines of this story do not belong to me.

These are our words and we will share them together.

PART ONE

August

The Unknown

CHAPTER ONE

Gentle Things

'Your relationships are shaping the experience of life'

Wednesday 1 August

If relationship breakups were a martial art, I'd be a black belt.

I've had way too much practice at heartbreak. I'm a 38-year-old man, hopefully not even halfway through my life. Yet I've experienced enough heartbreak to last 10 lifetimes. It occurs to me that I have never dumped someone. That includes my first long-term teenage relationship.

I can't believe I've lost Astrid. I love her so much. I don't know what to do next.

I'm worried for my two beautiful daughters too. They don't deserve this. Someone told me recently that the only people who experience the grace of unconditional love are our children. I guess I've learnt that the hard way.

Jessica and Haylie are my world. Without them, I'd be consumed with darkness. They are the only reason I remain coherent at this stage. I'm so worried for them. They've gone through this sort of thing too often for kids so young. My relationship with their mother ended six years ago. But before that happened, we broke up often during our time together. Like a lot of parental relationships, we always got back together for the sake of the children.

I never thought it would happen with Astrid though. I can see, in Jess and Haylie's eyes, exactly the same repetitive heartbreak I feel within myself. Recognising their despair leaves me more desperate, because I can't protect them from it.

I feel ashamed that I allowed my job to get in the way of everything. I realise that the pressure from work was taxing Astrid but I didn't see this coming. I feel lied to. If I'm honest, I have to admit that most of the time I feel angry. My job is difficult. It is a high-pressure thing with lots of responsibility. I feel abandoned. Astrid bailed when things got tough.

I understand that I allowed the stress of my work to take hold, and that made things difficult. But I was just trying to do my best. Astrid knew I was going through a difficult time. We told each other we would be together forever. I feel like I've lost part of my identity.

I've decided to take an extended break from work. I couldn't possibly manage the workload at the moment. In fact, the idea of facing anything is overwhelming. I feel lost, I can't see past the darkness. And the whole thing is all too familiar.

On top of all of that, I feel too embarrassed to face my family and friends. I don't know how to explain this to them. The truth of what happened makes me feel small.

The fact that it keeps happening makes me feel like a failure.

So let's sum up at the end of my first night of this thing.

I was getting slammed at work and didn't handle the pressure very well. I ignored Astrid to the extent that she left. I can't breathe properly; I've never felt this hurt. And I have no idea how to usher my two daughters, who are innocent bystanders, through the current situation.

I am completely lost in my thoughts. I have no idea who I am any more. I feel like I need to get out of my own skin. I feel ashamed. I find myself showering several times a day just to get away from myself. And it looks like I am going to face all of these problems with the uncertainty of being a single parent who has to pay the bills without an income.

Well played Simon. Great job!

Thursday

I've never felt this low. I can barely get out of bed in the morning. Checking the mail is overwhelming. And eating doesn't seem to help the empty feeling I have in the pit of my stomach. I'm so sick of knowing exactly what a relationship breakup looks like.

As soon as you lose someone you love, you instantly stop taking the little things for granted. Somehow, you love things with more intensity. But it doesn't bring peace. It just adds to the desperation. All I want to do is close the curtains and sit in the dark. But the people close to me won't allow that to happen. My support people Tristan, Bryce, my sister Nicola and my folks, rub my shoulder or hold my elbow and say things like:

'You just need to look after yourself now; it's time to put yourself first.'

So, because I'm devoured with confusion, I engage in things with a constant haze of heaviness. I feel disconnected and vague during everyday activities. The centre of my being feels like a stagnant pool of water. Hope is the only thing I have to lose. And I've had enough of pinning everything on hope. I'm tired of wishing my way through life.

The only thing that got me out of bed today was the idea of writing. I have decided to write to myself every day. I am going to have a conversation with myself here, and I don't intend to hold anything back. I need tangible things (verbs) to help me through this process. Without action, I think I might lose myself all together. The familiarity of heartbreak is honestly buckling my psyche.

In my job as a Child Protection Officer, one of the tasks is to write daily case notes on the children we work with. The notes are a summary of what is going on for them. Writing case notes helps keep things clear and fresh. It adds retrospective certainty to the job.

I have decided to write a daily account of what I am going through. I don't know what else to do. I don't want to be familiar with each stage of a relationship breakdown. I'm tired of this nine-to-five, smartphone distracting, underwhelming life.

I want things to be different. It's time to own my part in what keeps happening with my intimate relationships. I don't want to be an expert in heartbreak. I don't want to simply hope my way through life any more. I know that writing helps unpack what's going on with language. That sort of deliberate intent brings clarity. I am going to write about my experience. I need to understand how to stop it from happening all the time.

In opening a dialogue, I am intentionally bringing retrospective certainty to what I'm going through. Often, that can be the start of understanding things a little better. Understanding what's happening gives everything a gentle accent. And I want gentle things. I'm going to have a conversation with myself here. And because I am the only audience member, I have nothing to lose. I will write as if I'm the reader. I will communicate without inhibitions.

Hopes and dreams seem to have me looking up at the stars. During difficult times, I find myself standing outside looking up in silence. I always hope God is paying attention. I find myself going to bed wishing for a miracle. I'm not here to dismiss hopes and dreams, but it's time to add intention to them.

I don't know what else I'm meant to do.

Friday

Happiness can be a simple thing.

Jess and Haylie show me that all the time. Today I remembered the importance of sharing with others. I spent the day talking with two of my closest friends. Tristan and Bryce are amazing guys. They are steady, deliberate men. And their wisdom always offers a lighter perspective on things.

I know the pressures from work had a massive impact on what happened with Astrid. I have worked with Tristan and Bryce for over 10 years. They are appropriate people to confide in about the pressures I faced because they witnessed them first hand.

Looking back, I realise they saw the impact work was having on my private life. Unfortunately, I was blind to the enormity of what was going on. And that oblivion has cost me a great deal. I find comfort in the support of others because at the moment I'm in shock.

So I need to trust the people I trust.

After talking with the guys I realised a lot. For the past two years I felt overwhelmed by my job. I understand now that I didn't deal with that appropriately. I did what I've always done… I looked for isolation. More significantly, I turned away from Astrid and got caught up in the internal struggle of the whole thing. I convinced myself the stress of the job was important.

However, I realised today that the pressure goes much deeper than simple rumination. For a long time now, Tristan and Bryce have been warning me about taking on too much. I always ignored them because I didn't understand. Their chief concern was that I'm quick to take on other people's problems. Today they gently confronted my own self-worth, and challenged me to check what I get from fighting other people's battles.

Initially, I was frustrated because I didn't see the connection between my self-worth and helping others. If someone needs my help they generally get it. I didn't understand how the idea of helping someone converted to the fact that I didn't feel worthy. Bryce asked what I got from taking on other people's problems.

Interestingly, I couldn't answer him.

Not being able to answer sharpened my awareness and revealed a blinding truth. As quick as a thought is created, I saw the cycle of negativity I had created for myself. The truth is, taking on other people's problems is what I've always done. That's what keeps me up at night. I am addicted to the struggle of my internal dialogue. I've been a martyr. I've been a self-defeating martyr so that I don't have to face myself. I take on other people's problems so that I don't have to face my life. I'm trying to prove something to myself here. I constantly seek isolation so that I don't have to look at my place in the world. I have been relying on the drama of my life.

And I'm weary. I've had enough of it. I want something much simpler. I want to learn how to fall asleep without being consumed by worry. Instead of sitting in silence, allowing the struggle to be my only comfort, I want to relax.

I want to feel the warmth of love. I want to know what it feels like to turn to intimacy, instead of being philosophically in my head all of the time. I want to learn how to show affection during difficult times. I want to walk away from the constant isolation of my life.

I just want happiness to be simple.

Saturday

In a lot of ways, I'm worried this is not rock bottom. I woke this morning feeling lifeless. I couldn't feel my body as I walked to the bathroom to have a shower. My face seemed heavy. My shoulders were slumped with resignation. I looked at my reflection in the mirror. There was nothing but sorrow staring back at me. My eyes looked dim. I saw a reflection of heartbreak. My eyes told a story of sorrow.

Everything with Astrid ended so quickly.

It feels like our breakup was not meant to be somehow. I understand I was lazy. I get that my actions hurt her. But understanding all of that isn't helping. I still feel blindsided by everything. Dealing with heartbreak feels a bit like being in a lifeboat in the middle of the nothingness of an ocean. Every day I wake up and look around. I feel trapped by the inability to change my circumstance. The ocean that encircles me is nothing more than the status quo.

I honestly thought Astrid and I were meant to build a life together. Surely providence can't be bumped off course. I can't help but think that what's currently happening was not meant to be part of the cosmic plan. But how can destiny get body-slammed!

I cling to hope, but I'm also not sure if I'm meant to surrender to the feeling of regret. I've never understood regret until now.

I play golf sometimes.

Lord knows the game of golf could be a fitting metaphor for regret. Just like being in an intimate relationship, history indicates that I don't know what I'm doing when I play the game. As bad as I am though, I have always owned my lack of ability. I've never understood why so many recreational golfers spend time talking about what could have happened if things were different. They waste so much energy talking about the ifs-buts-and-maybes of their game. Essentially, they pay no attention to what is actually happening. They play the entire game in their heads, thinking and wishing things were better.

In my mind, focusing on what could have happened and then complaining about the fact that it didn't is the same as regret. Living a life with self-imposed regret has never made any sense to me. When deliberate action causes someone to lay down if-but-and-maybes in order to feel better, all I see is self-imposed limitation.

I don't normally spend much time wondering about what could have happened. For me, the things in life that are meant to be are easy to recognise. All you have to do is look at what took place.

And yet, part of me feels like everything I just wrote is nothing more than a sonnet.

Because here I sit at two o'clock in the morning, feeling a profound sense of regret for the first time. I don't know if what Astrid and I are going through is a separation or a breakup. However, I can say without a moment's hesitation, if our relationship is destroyed because I treated it with apathy, I'll regret it for the rest of my life.

It doesn't make sense that God's plan (providence) gets body-slammed by my first experience of regret.

There's no way regret trumps destiny.

Yet here I am, reflecting in the middle of the night, wishing I could scrub this feeling off me. This has to be what rock bottom feels like.

Sunday

Lots of people are telling me to take it easy lately. Quite frankly I don't understand what that means. Do they want me to drink herbal tea or something? Maybe I'm meant to go swimming with dolphins. I'm feeling quite angry today and I have no desire to stifle that. However, I want to be clear with myself. I'm not attacking the people who are trying to help. I understand they're just worried, and they are doing their best to get me through a difficult situation.

I find myself looking up from what I write as I consider the idea of taking it easy.

Maybe I'm meant to go to bed early and get a good night's sleep. The thing is, if I could ignore my internal dialogue and rest peacefully I wouldn't be in this predicament. At this stage I'd be willing to give up ice cream for a little peace of mind.

Perhaps I'm meant to lean on the people who care. Maybe some of their advice is right. Perhaps all I need to do is get back out there and put my worries behind me. But when you feel like this you want to be left alone. I want people (other than Jess and Haylie) to get away from me. Going out and being social is about as appealing as exercising with a hangover.

'Just take it easy Simon'

If I could do that, there would be no reason for people to say it in the first place. I would love to ignore everything that's happened and simply relax. My inability to take it easy is what has landed me in this mess to begin with.

It almost seems ironic that my relationship with Astrid broke down because I was consumed with worry and doubt. Weirdly, my problems before now seem insignificant. I dropped all of my previous concerns without even trying. Yet, at one point, they were so huge that they broke Astrid and me. If my concerns were potent enough to break love then where the hell did they go!

I'd really like to know what looking after yourself looks like when you're struggling.

One of my main problems is that I've lost Astrid's trust. She won't talk to me. Life would be a lot easier if she would answer her bloody phone, or return a text message. It seems as if she has completely given up on us. I am losing hope very quickly. The uncertainty about our future is suffocating. The noise of doubt has never been louder. And the best advice I'm getting at the moment is to take it easy.

Awesome. No problem. I'll just hug a friggin' puppy or something.

Monday

The most difficult thing to handle is the nonstop noise of my thoughts.

I almost deafened myself when I started the car today. The radio was so loud, I instinctively smacked the driver's side window when the stereo came on. After recovering from the sonic boom, I realised just how overpowering my internal dialogue is. Evidently, my thoughts are so distracting I need the stereo turned up four million decibels just to hear the music.

Everything is so tiring. My jaw is clenched all of the time. My shoulders are pent-up. And my eyes are constantly resisting me. Every time there is a slight noise, I check my phone in a panic to see if it's Astrid calling me. The times I actually do manage to pay attention, I feel heavy about everything. When you walk with heartbreak it feels like you're getting shorter with every step.

I didn't sleep well again last night. The first thing I thought about after waking was this dialogue. It's strange. I don't really know what's happening. But I feel compelled to do this thing. I can't say I look forward to writing every day. It's not like I hang out for it. But at the same time, reflecting in this manner brings a weird kind of substance to the day.

It's difficult to explain. I think it might have something to do with being honest with myself. Unpacking what's going on in such a structured way is offering something I haven't experienced before. And truth be told, I have no idea what I'm attempting to explain to myself here.

As I said, it must be about unpacking stuff honestly. With that in mind I shall push on.

Friday was a big day. I woke to the self-defeating martyr I created. It's quite a thing to recognise the small aspects of your own personality. It's both empowering and confronting. I finally saw the strain I had placed on myself. I also realised I'm bringing that reality to everything else. I was so unhappy and angry about my professional life. The strain infiltrated everything. What I'm referring to here is why Astrid left.

And enough is enough.

I've decided things are going to change. I will make what's happening a life-changing event. I will not allow what I'm going through to be a simple relationship breakdown that will get better with time. I will make the events of the past week the start of something different. I've had enough of living small.

I'm a long way from better. I'm nowhere close to healed. In fact, heartbreak and anger still ambush me every day. There is an aspect of my personality that will always be a little tenacious. I understand that. But tenacity doesn't have to define me. I don't have to be measured by extremes any more. I can accept that sometimes life is difficult without letting that consume me.

Constantly worrying has cost me too much. I'm tired of what I've always done. The strain I have placed on everything feels small. It honestly makes my eyes narrow when I look back on it. I consciously choose to drop the struggle out of my life. Things are going to be different.

And as I close off for the night, let me emphasise what I keep hearing:

'There's a gift to be had here'

There's something to remember. Our relationships are shaping the experience of life.

CHAPTER TWO

Trust Love

'Life is not what you think. You are more than what you think about. You are most certainly more than your doubts.'

Tuesday

There is a major difference between communicating what you don't want, versus what you actually do. One statement is a direct line to honesty. The other is about avoidance.

I want new beginnings.

I don't know how to live differently, but I'm not going to allow the unknown of that to stop me. When I think about changing how I operate, I can't help but think about my kids. Since Jess and Haylie started living with me every other week, I have been uncompromising with my parenting style. I constantly look through the eyes of a life-coach. I am defined by reliability.

That's a noble virtue, and I will always be available for my children. But I recognise that if I'm weary of my own life, I must be bringing that to them. Being a parent is part of who I am. It is part of my heart's work. If I'm serious about addressing where I've come from, then I have to look at my parenting.

I can't believe I'm about to admit this. But I think I have a stranglehold on my parenting style. Always striving to be a better Dad separates me from being a relaxing influence. Always looking through the eyes of a life-coach is tiring. I'm sick of the whole thing. And if I'm honest, I bet my kids are weary too.

What I am referring to here is an extension of the struggle of my life. I'm tired of being an unrelenting father. I want something a lot simpler. I am going to let go of the stranglehold I've brought to my parenting. It's time to relax into the love I share with Jess and Haylie. It's time to trust that without reservation.

In fact, I'm going to drop the stranglehold I've got on all of the aspects of my life. I'm tired deep in my bones. Maniacally living in my head is finished. I'm not sure what's going to happen next. I think it's going to have something to do with living my highest reality. My instincts tell me that it's time to wake up here. Simplifying things is about trusting something bigger than myself.
It starts by trusting a higher purpose. It's time to drop what I've always done and embrace the unknown.

Dare I say it, but maybe it's time to trust love.

And I have absolutely no idea why I just wrote that.

I haven't got the faintest clue where all of that came from. I sound like my mother. I'm not a religious guy, but I guess I'm quite spiritual. Having a mother who's a clairvoyant, and a father who believes in the Creative Force of the Universe, probably meant that I was always going to be quite spiritual.

For reasons I can't explain, I know that as I go through this process, my higher purpose will be revealed. And as I sit here now, I have no idea why I keep hearing that.

Except to say that it must have something to do with letting go.

If things are complicated it's because I complicate them. My higher purpose has got something to do with getting out of my own way. When I contemplate what that actually looks like, I instinctively think about Jess and Haylie. Perhaps dropping the stranglehold I have on our relationship is about trusting in something much bigger. Maybe letting go is linked to my higher purpose because both realities involve trusting love.

Equal to that, perhaps not knowing what I'm saying or what's coming next is the entire point. Maybe the unknown holds all the answers.

Wednesday

I did something pretty radical.

I got tattoos on each of my wrists. I understand that one of the first rules about going through a relationship breakup is that you never get tattoos about it. Normally, it's a huge mistake because you always move on. It was a manic thing to do, but that's exactly why I got them. I deliberately went over the top and branded myself so I never forget.

The tattoos are two Bible passages. Each, for separate reasons, has always meant a great deal to me. As I mentioned yesterday, I am not a religious guy. I don't rely on that to find answers. However, I also flat-out refuse to knock religion. Too many people do that already. I've never understood why one person's truth automatically means invalidating someone else's. I marked myself for spiritual reasons, not religious ones.

> *'Religion that God our Father accepts as pure and faultless is this: To look after our orphans and widows in their distress and to keep oneself from being polluted by the world.'*
> James 1:27

That passage is precisely why I chose to work with at-risk children. All those years ago, I chose my career-path because of that quote. I wanted a job that was meaningful. It was about the challenge. I wanted to do something that most other people wouldn't take on. And I couldn't think of anything more meaningful than working with kids that were difficult to reach.

James 1:27 is a noble thing. It represents a life of service and dedication. However, it also serves as a reminder of the struggle I put myself through. Not because caring for others is arduous, but because I allowed myself to become polluted by the experience. And allowing that to happen was a showstopper.

> *'Love bears all things, believes all things, hopes all things, endures all things.'*
> 1 Corinthians 13:7

I had a Catholic upbringing. I've read the Bible from one end to the other. People can say what they want about the Bible and religion. I choose to make them about love. 1st Corinthians 13:7 sums it up perfectly. The passage represents the exact philosophy I want to reach. It is the ethos I want for Jess and Haylie. It's what I hope for Astrid. The message is simple and clear. It is faultless in every way.

'Love is everything'

Getting heartbreak tattoos is normally not a great idea. It is a reactive indelible thing to do. Time has a way of making things better, and you risk eventually regretting the decision. But I feel comforted by them. They represent what's possible. Each message serves as a reminder. I have looked at them accidentally several times today, and have felt optimistic every time. Having the imagery so close to my hands helps me feel strong. Contemplating each passage leaves me feeling gentle.

And from now on, I will constantly be reminded of those things. It will be the domain from which I operate as I move forward. Not because something happened to me though. Branding my body was not about something happening to me. The tattoos don't hold magical powers.

Feeling gentle and comforted is a choice. Recognising the peace of each message is about waking up. It's a conscious choice, brought about from an indelible peace of imagery. The domain from which I will operate is now in my hands whenever I choose it to be.

I choose to recognise the gentle influence of love.

Thursday

I finally know what taking it easy means.

As I said the other day, I've never understood that sentiment. But now I finally understand the substance behind the idea. To say that I had an amazing day would be a massive understatement. Today was one of the most incredible days I've ever had. Because of today, I'll always know what it means to look after myself. I finally understand it on a practical level.

Before I unpack what happened, I need to emphasise something. One of the good things about deliberately accepting, and looking for change, is that a lot of what happens is an x-factor. For me at least, some of what I'm going through resides in the unspoken world. Most of what's happening is new. Because that's true, it's also quite difficult to unpack sometimes. The very nature of an x-factor means it's tough to explain. If it were easy, it wouldn't be what we call it.

For some reason I understood something about the unexplainable that has changed everything. Embracing the unknown was brilliant today. I no longer feel lost and heavy. Light entered my world and I feel new.

This is what happened.

I was cooking dinner. As always, I was distracted by my thoughts. I was thinking about how much I miss Astrid. I was also worried about my job prospects. I found myself questioning almost everything that's happened recently. I started to get bogged down by it again. I could feel the tension in my jaw growing. I became aware of the stress in my shoulders and neck. I found myself thumping and slapping things around the kitchen as I cooked.

I was in the all too familiar place of anger and resentment again. The noise of doubt was deafening. Without intending to, I abruptly whacked our kitchen bench and told myself to shut up. I said it out loud and with forthright conviction. I literally blurted out 'shut up!' And then much to my surprise, there was silence.

And I mean that literally. Everything stopped. I found myself looking around. It was the most profound type of silence I had ever experienced. And yet, the stillness remained familiar. There was no noise in my head. My thoughts were gone, and all that was left was the peace of the moment. Not only was my head quiet, I could literally see the stillness with my eyes.

Everything was brighter and so much cleaner. I connected with a type of awareness that was new, but also familiar. It was fresh and untouched. But somehow the awareness had always been there. In a split second, I saw life without clutter. A light replaced the pollution of my negative thoughts.

I saw everything without the presence of thought. A relaxed feeling of atonement washed over me. And I was filled with gentle excitement. The relief I felt was new, but if it's possible, I had been there before. Without knowing how, I conceptualised the innocence in the stillness of the moment.

I saw in one breath, that the innocence of life has always been there. I finally understood that the purest sense of life is not conceived from thought.

This is what I know without question.

There is an everlasting force that sits beneath our daily distractions. This new awareness brings choice to everything. You no longer have to be ruled by your thoughts. They are simply one aspect of your experience. Life is not what you think. You are more than what you think about. You are most certainly more than your doubts. Taking it easy means choosing to stop listening to your negative self-talk. It means not breathing in the pollution of your distractions.

Looking after myself is about recognising that I am not what I tell myself during the difficult times. I can choose to step outside the pollution of my doubts and view life with fresh eyes. I can sit in the stillness of the moment and understand the peace I feel comes from seeing my thoughts for what they are. They are simply my thoughts. They are quite simply one point of view. And they no longer have to rule my experience.

The Unknown

After I saw beyond the pollution of my thoughts everything became brighter. The silence of life has never been louder. There is a celestial light beneath the creation of your thoughts. This light is everywhere and it always has been.

I know it sounds strange, but the simple fact is, I saw a light in everything that can never be touched. I saw an aspect of life that stretches far beyond the horizon. I felt a type of liberation like no other. Not only did the noise of my doubts disappear, but I also saw the silence with my own eyes. I saw the stillness everywhere. And my reality was filled with light.

And then I quite simply took it easy.

Friday

Whoa, yesterday was huge!

I detached from the potency of my thoughts. I saw for the first time that life was not what you think. It was so refreshing to detach from the negative cycle of my internal dialogue. There is a clean, uncomplicated awareness in the silence of my internal world.

Yesterday, I knew that things were going to be okay. I conceptualised peace of mind. Today, I conducted myself from a place of stillness. I spoke without reacting to my thoughts. I listened without judgment, and communicated free from expectation. I engaged in different activities without distraction. What happened next was a freaking Coke commercial. Thank God!

From now on, I'm not going to talk about things being better at some point in the future. It's time to accept that my life is beneath my feet now. This is the path of my reality. It is here and I'm ready. Things are going to be okay because they are already. Even if I think that's not true, it doesn't really matter. My doubts and worries can take a back seat. I address the intent of my life for something bigger than the noise of doubt.

And I have to admit, I'm amazed how quickly things are happening. So much has happened in a short time. The momentum of the past couple of days is maxed out. I'm certain that engaging in this dialogue is part of the reason. Unpacking what I'm going through with self-reflection is adding a timeless aspect to my life.

I remember watching an interview with a guy who had a near-death experience. At the point of death, he felt a huge relief because it was the first occasion he noticed an existence that wasn't measured by time. It reminds me of the past couple of days. Yesterday, I saw an existence that is not measured by time. Noticing the stillness in life feels a bit like detaching from time.

Sounds completely weird. I don't know what's going on. All I know right now is that I am more than my thoughts. From the stillness of the moment, I understand that my doubts are not going to be the things that ultimately define me.

THE UNKNOWN

Once I accept that, I start to understand the choice in life. There is a type of consciousness that is separate to what I think.

I have woken up to a part of my psyche that is always still.

I would keep writing but I feel compelled to stop. I guess sometimes there are simply no words. And trust me when I say acknowledging that is a very big step for me. I'm stopping here tonight because I want to silence my words. The stillness waits. I'll finish up by emphasising this: somehow there is a part of us that is timeless.

And the light to that reality echoes forever.

CHAPTER THREE

Snowflake of the Moment

'When things are complete in your life, even the hardest moments are cleaner and easier to recognise.'

Saturday

And whack!

Like a frying pan to the face. I swear, every time I start to get ahead of myself, life has a way of slamming on the brakes. There was a part of me that actually thought I didn't have a right to this sort of happiness. A small unspoken part of me thought it was too soon to feel so good. I also started to feel like my happiness was cheating on Astrid somehow. Despite everything that's happened over the past week, I started to feel a little stressed. I noticed my eyes straining. It felt like I was leaving Astrid behind.

Consequently, with all of my newfound wisdom, I decided to contact her. And needless to say, I was faced with the manic nature of what's happening lately. The ups and downs are extreme to say the least. Yesterday I said that everything is going to be okay because it is already. Well that's difficult to accept today.

I tried to contact Astrid because I wanted to explain what's been happening recently. But she refused to answer her phone. So with all of my Yoda-like wisdom, I decided to ring several times throughout the day. I was determined to show her (through seeing my missed calls) that I wasn't giving up on us.

After several unanswered calls, she sent this text: 'Sorry I can't talk to you at the moment. I just need to look after myself now.'

Like a frying pan to the face.

When I look at our situation objectively, I understand why she has completely shut me out. It's not because I deserve it, or because she is being selfish. Astrid has 100 per cent bailed because she is heartbroken too. On an emotional level, I left her long before she moved out. All she knows of me is what I showed her.

The truth is, Astrid absolutely loved the girls and me. She gave so much of herself to our family. She tried to talk to me about our problems but I ignored her. I've pushed her away because I emotionally abandoned her ages ago. I want a chance to explain. I'd give anything for her to see that things will be different. But she won't even talk to me.

I'm starting to think it's over. I think it must be. That makes me sad because I get a sense that Jess, Haylie and I are on a path of emotional evolution together. It's deflating to consider that Astrid won't share that with us. The lack of contact is reinforcing just how sad she must be. As it stands, Astrid thinks I am lost in my work. She's convinced I'm not interested in her. In fact, she probably thinks I'm still working, facing the same old problems.

I refuse to text her about everything that has happened lately. I want to talk to her. I want her to hear me. What I've got to say is way too important to put in an electric message. It's too personal for that sort of trite crap. It's really difficult to stay out of my head today. I feel quite desperate actually. I'm not going to do anything with that though. The desperation of heartbreak is difficult enough. I certainly don't need to add to it.

Interestingly, all of the things I have experienced over the past week feel flimsy in this mindset. Everything I've written feels disingenuous. The potency of my experience feels like a lie in this current headspace of doubt.

I think I've lost her.

THE UNKNOWN

Sunday

A clean slate is as unique as a snowflake.

Everything seems heightened when you go through a relationship breakdown. It reminds me of the importance of paying attention. It's a humbling thing to lose someone you love so much. I find myself paying closer attention to the things that matter.

I've been busy with a lot of hands-on stuff lately. It feels good to keep busy. I'm cautious not to make it at the cost of paying attention though. I want to notice what I'm going through so I can change my outlook. I feel like I'm clearing a lot of the clutter from my life. I'm not referring to a cosmic thing when I say that. I am literally cleaning up a lot of things. I am completing things I've been ignoring for whatever reason. There is no procrastination in my world at the moment.

The whole process is therapeutic. Looking for completion is synchronised with changing your circumstance. There is something virtuous about starting each day with a clean slate. The unknown can be a little daunting sometimes. Being complete with things is helping when it comes to paying attention to what matters.

When things are complete in your life, even the hardest moments are cleaner and easier to recognise.

However, I'm finding something distracting and it's time to deal with it. I can't get past the fact that Astrid won't talk to me. Having no line of communication with her is difficult to accept. The progress I have made lately is stunted every time I think about her. I can't see the stillness in anything today.

I am reminded that when there is a lack of acceptance about something, it is difficult to detach from the potency of your thoughts. The lack of acceptance creates recurring thought patterns. Those thoughts turn into doubt all too easily. I'm finding it very difficult to move on. So much about Astrid remains doubtful.

Quite obviously, I remain incomplete and distracted by the finality of our breakup. It's time to clean up the lack of communication. I haven't pushed the issue because I don't want to lose hope for us. Hope is the only thing I have left when it comes to our relationship.

Looking for completion with different things is therapeutic when embracing the unknown. But having a clean slate can't only be about chores and tactile stuff.

In order to view each day with fresh eyes, I have to make sure my internal world is clean as well. I see now that I have to remove the clutter of my relationship breakdown. I can't continue to move forward until I deal with the fact that Astrid left so abruptly.

I'm going to try, perhaps for the last time, to contact her. If she ignores me again I'm pretty sure I will let it go once and for all.

Tonight, I put hope on the line.

Monday

My nephew Jack was born roughly 16 years ago. My sister Nicola had a home-birth. I was one of her support people. Mum and I stayed at Nic's house in Dwellingup after Jack was born. A few days after the birth, Mum and Nic started talking about psychic things. This was not unusual for them. Mum is a clairvoyant. Talking about intuitive things is normal in our family.

They were talking about what their futures looked like. I was sitting quietly reading. Initially, I was not involved in the conversation. That sort of thing was not normally on my radar, not really something I paid much attention to.
I reside in the 'what are the Lotto numbers world' when it comes to psychic stuff.

I can't actually remember why, but I broke protocol and got involved in the conversation. I started asking all the normal questions. What does my future look like, will I meet someone, be successful and find happiness. I distinctly remember asking if my life would ever make sense.

Both Mum and Nic answered by saying that at some stage in the future, I would find myself at the beach. They explained that I would be looking out at the ocean, taking it all in. I was told in that precise moment I would feel the peace and atonement of nature. Coming from that place, not only would my life start to make sense, but everything else would fall into place as well. They explained intuitively, that I would experience the strength of connection in everything.

Today was amazing.

I sat with real excitement when I remembered that conversation. Although I'm retelling it now, I had actually forgotten about it until tonight. I've been to the beach lots of times in Jack's life. And yet, tonight was the first time I remembered the beach moment conversation.

I organised to go to the beach tonight. It wasn't until I was just about to pull into Hillarys Boat Harbour that I remembered what I was told. I knew straight away the Creative Forces of the Universe were at play. Because at exactly the moment I remembered the conversation, Mum called my mobile.

She was just checking in with me. I told her where I was, and reminded her of the conversation we had all those years ago. She wished me luck and told me to remain emotionally still. She reminded me to pay attention. What Mum and Nic didn't tell me 16 years ago was that someone else would be there with me.

I finally got through to Astrid. After a short phone conversation she agreed to see me. We decided to meet at the beach where we shared our first sunset together. I told her as much as I've come to realise. I spoke from the heart. I owned my part in the dismantling of our relationship. We've got a long way to go but it's a start. Tonight I drove home with a glimmer of hope.

Regardless of what happens, Mum and Nicola were right. It took close to two decades, but they were precisely right. I understand exactly what direction my life will take. Everything is finally starting to make sense. Tonight, for a moment that will be with me forever, I understood the sunset.

Tuesday

The Creative Force of the Universe is incredible.

So as it turns out, we're not our feelings either. And I'm not even sure what that means yet. I haven't conceptualised it. But nevertheless, our true nature sits beneath the expression of our feelings.

Today I experienced lots of random little miracles. I started the day by relaxing into the moment. I planned nothing and ended up cleaning all day. The thing is, the house wasn't that messy to begin with. It became obvious that I was clearing the house, rather than just cleaning it. And I don't even know what that means. It doesn't matter though. It's precisely what I did. I kept going to make a list of things to buy. I wanted a few little things for different rooms. Weird thing is, every time I thought of something, it literally showed up.

Here are a few examples: Firstly, I was detail-cleaning the laundry. I was completely devoted to the moment. Coming from nothing, it occurred to me that a plastic tub would be good for all of the cleaning products. As that idea came to me, I was putting something in the spare room. And sitting in the middle of the floor (as obvious as can be) was an empty plastic tub.

Not long after that, I had just finished cleaning the bathrooms. I was standing in the doorway of the main bathroom appreciating how clean and complete it looked. I decided at some stage to buy a couple of small stereos so that we could listen to music while we're getting ready every day. At that precise moment, I felt deep warmth for our home.

Wanting to ride the wave of appreciation, I decided to face something I'd been putting off. It was time to re-organise the walk-in wardrobe in my bedroom. Obviously, all of Astrid's clothes and shoes are gone. I have felt incomplete looking at a half-empty closet every day. It was a constant reminder that she left. And I decided to clean up that reality.

As soon as I started moving some of my clothes around, I found two unopened Christmas presents for the girls. I unwrapped them out of curiosity and sure enough, the gifts were two small docking-station stereos that obviously didn't make it under the tree last Christmas. I guess Astrid bought them. Now the bathrooms have music. And it seems like it came from a feeling of appreciation.

Finally, I had an old big-screen plasma TV that's been sitting in the backyard for the past year. I pushed it out the front so I could sweep. Later in the day I was cleaning the kitchen cupboards. I was completely devoted to the moment. I was literally finding the joy in the simple act of cleaning. I saw the snowflake of the moment.

Coming from that place, I intuitively pictured getting rid of the TV. I didn't think about it, I simply accepted the satisfaction of it being gone. Before anything else happened, a guy knocked on the door (after seeing the TV out the front of the house) and asked if it was up for grabs.

Those sort of random little miracles happened all day. It was so cool. Embracing the unknown starts with clearing things up. It comes from cleaning your life. It's almost as if the Creative Force of the Universe sits beneath the noise of life.

It seems to be waiting on common ground.

Wednesday

Experiencing random little miracles…

I'm not suggesting the Creative Force of the Universe is about getting cool stuff. I'm not here to convince myself of that. There's no depth in that line of thinking. Assuming that it's only about validation is a limiting idea. Feeling a connection with something beyond your imagination is not about getting cool stuff all the time. It's about trusting in something bigger. It's about daring to believe that you are bigger than the noise of your preoccupations. It is a type of awareness that sits beneath your feelings.

Today was awesome. I felt completely grounded and present all day. Late in the afternoon, I instinctively felt grateful about seeing Astrid two nights ago. I noticed a feeling of gratitude that was sparked from a sense of hope for us. I didn't expect anything from what I was feeling, and therefore it was cloaked in certainty.

I felt my eyes starting to shine.

And then Astrid showed up to say hello. We spoke for a little while. She said she was happy to see me the other night. She talked about needing some time and space to figure things out. She spoke gently and with intent. Before she left, Astrid told me that I seemed somehow familiar to her. She sounded comforted. For the first time in a long while, there was something meaningful between us. And I was reminded of how the little things matter the most sometimes. I remembered just how simple happiness could be.

Today was quite simply amazing. As I sit here now, I understand that the feeling I have comes from expecting nothing. I was not attached to an outcome at any stage today. I just accepted the unknown. There is something familiar about the unknown. There is an unknown aspect to all of life that has always been there. It is a type of stillness that is beneath our thoughts and feelings.

Today, I did my best to notice the stillness in everything. It might sound a little corny but the day felt like the sound a sword makes when it cuts through the air. That's exactly what it felt like to devote myself to the moment. There is a compelling sharpness to everything when you step outside the pollution of your thoughts.

After the recent events, I feel compelled to ask myself this: what if God is more than what we've been taught? What would it look like if the Creative Force of the Universe was more than we have imagined. I'm not suggesting God exists because I got cool stuff over the past couple of days. I'm referring to living in the moment. I'm talking about recognising the stillness that is detached from my thoughts.

The past few days I have connected with the stillness of the moment. And this is what I found there: bliss, joy, fulfilment, trust, peace, abundance, connection, unity, warmth, excitement, love.

Those virtues are entirely about the Creative Force of the Universe. I'm pretty sure we're talking about God here.

In fact I'm certain we are.

Thursday

I was up late again last night. As soon as I woke today, I thought about this dialogue. I rushed through the morning routine so that I could pick up where I left off. Engaging in this conversation has been amazing. I am connected to a type of motivation that is difficult to describe. What's going on here feels bigger than anything I have taken on before.

I don't believe in coincidence and chance happenings. Knowing all things have a purpose leaves me mystified about what I'm going through. On my best day, in my cleanest moment, I am just leaving myself alone. I am trying not to add too much to the experience. Simply observing your life adds substance to everything.

I believe God is omnipresent. Which is to say, God is everything and everywhere. Rather than giving energy to coincidence, I believe in cause and effect. Everything has a purpose, and all things come with consequence. The motion of cause and effect is an unstoppable force.

And I just love the effect this dialogue is causing.

A lot of what is happening here is about cleaning my life. Connecting with the possibilities of God is about being willing to look with fresh eyes. It's about meeting that reality on common ground. I guess it would be a little difficult to look into the Creative Force of the Universe authentically if I'm busy pretending I know everything in the first place. There's nothing clean about that outlook. That reality is not about embracing the unknown.

Choosing to go after completion is about observation. It's about recognising the things in your life that need to be addressed so that you can move forward with a clean slate. That's what it means to see the snowflake of the moment.

Friday

I guess most people would define me as agnostic, because I don't connect with a formal religion. But in truth, I don't see myself that way. I spend no time questioning what (or who) God is. My heart tells me that God is everything. As I stipulated yesterday, I believe God is omnipresent. My truth is that there is no place She is not. There is no irrefutable form or energy-source that God cannot take on.

'God is Life.'

Before I go on, I will emphasise that I have no problem referring to God as a female or male. Further to that, I see no separation between the Creative Force of the Universe and God. That's the reason I put the Creative Force of the Universe in capital letters. This is my story, and that's how I choose to respect the Creator of all things.

In many respects, I'm here to rattle the spiritual cage. I'm comfortable referring to God as a female because doing so serves to jolt me out of any preconceived ideas I have.

I've had enough of placing limits on things. I am sick of living small. I'm here to activate my highest reality. On my cleanest day, I use my authentic voice to do that. This is a process of identifying what makes me tick. This dialogue is about giving the anticipation of my insights a platform to explore things.

Recognising the snowflake of the moment is about trusting your insights. It's about acting upon what you hear from within for the purpose of growth. And tonight, this is what I hear from the stillness of choice:

'God cannot be contained by one description.'

CHAPTER FOUR

Emotional Stocktake

'Once you accept that your problems come from your thoughts, the unknown is really the only path you can take as you look to change direction.'

Saturday

I can't stop thinking about what happened on the ninth of August.

It is a moment (and a day) that will be with me forever. It was the stillness found there that woke me up. It's hard to believe it was only nine days ago. Since then, I haven't felt the same. I have found that validating the experience with language helps transfer it into reality. With that in mind, I feel compelled to talk about the liberation of detaching from the pollution of your thoughts.

I'm mindful that each time I have attempted to explain it, my descriptions have been quite lofty. I shall attempt to do it in a more grounded, protein-based manner.

Let's make it simple Simon.

Imagine you are struggling with something. Imagine dealing with something like heartbreak or stress. Normally during those times we turn to people for support. Most of us have a small network of support people. These guys are normally gentle and giving. It's not typical for them to be harsh during tough times.

Now, for the sake of this conversation, let's do something radical.

Imagine your thoughts become part of your support network. Imagine what you tell yourself is your very own support person. Your internal dialogue is a person who is trying to help. Your advice is your thoughts. Turn your thoughts into an imaginary person. Allow the influence of your thoughts to come to life within your imagination.

Bring to life all of your if-but-and-maybes. Wake up to all of your doubts by pretending they are true. Bring the non-stop noise of your internal dialogue alive. Realise that if you are in despair, it's because your thoughts have taken you there.

All of that shouldn't be too hard to imagine. Because the truth is, that's basically what we believe when times are tough. We believe that our doubts and worries are justified. We trust the noise of our thoughts. We see it as simply the truth about the problems we face. We believe something is happening to us against our will. When we're down, it's easy to believe we are victims. During a very stressful situation everything seems difficult. That defines what we call it. The problem is, our thoughts are not normally very helpful during those times.

Everything seems difficult because your thoughts make it so.

To clarify, imagine what you think, is a person who is constantly second-guessing everything. It's not a question of being wrong or bad though. The imaginary support person has your best interests at heart. That's why they are relentless. The fact is, your thoughts are your partner in despair. Literally.

On Thursday the ninth of August I realised that I had a choice. I can choose to ignore the negative self-talk. My negative dialogue is no more real than an imaginary person giving advice. I can choose not to listen to that stuff because I created it.

Understand that we are more than what we think about. Thoughts are generated from within, but they are not all there is. Recognising the stillness beneath your thoughts is entirely about seeing the creator of those things. Beneath the creation of your thoughts there is something much bigger, much simpler going on. And it's always resting peacefully. It is the part of your psyche that is connected to everything.

Detaching from the potency of your thoughts starts with recognising who created them. It's about waking up to something more. It's about tapping into the greatest version of who you are.

It's that simple Simon.

Sunday

Everything I've written lately has left me in a bit of a spin. I think I need to pull up for a second.

I'm almost startled by the pace of my so-called emotional development throughout the past couple of weeks. Things are happening incredibly fast. I think it's time for an emotional stocktake.

Part of me can't understand why I feel so content sometimes. Astrid moved out only a moment ago. Sometimes it seems too soon to feel this good. Being Astrid's man was one of the first things I identified with. As I sit here now, she's gone and our future is unclear. Part of me thinks I should be more desperate about losing her.

In addition to that, I seem to be getting further away from the success of my career. Caring for people who can't look after themselves is challenging. You have to want it. And I'm not sure I do any more. The ability to do the job well seems to be fading quickly. And yet, it used to bring me so much comfort. I was proud to be a Child Protection Officer. My career mattered. In fact, I allowed it to matter too much. I allowed the significance of it to become toxic. I hid behind the struggles I faced there.

When I think about Astrid leaving, and the fact that I left my career so quickly I get in touch with the gravity of everything that's changed recently. So much of what made me feel comfortable in the past is gone now. So much of what I thought mattered doesn't any more.

And the confusing thing is this: sometimes my level of comfort, in the face of so much uncertainty, is the very thing that makes me uncomfortable.

Monday

It's almost as if I am dealing with two realities.

It is clear that I am finding it difficult to move forward every day because I miss Astrid so much. As I sit here now, I take a quick deep breath. It's all a little bit tiring. In many ways, it's like I've only just woken up. When it comes to detaching from the potency of my thoughts, I feel like I'm wiping the sleep out of my eyes. Every time I anticipate explaining it, I feel like a fawn that's just found its legs.

I'm not referring to being unstable when I say that though. I feel fragile without being unstable. At least that's what it feels like to write about it. When it comes to exploring the stillness of the moment, I feel gently young. My spiritual eyes feel new. The anticipation of everything recently is exciting, and that's great. But I also feel disappointed sometimes because of the lack of Astrid in my life.

Mostly, I've been able to leave myself alone during those moments. Which is a great emotional-muscle to flex for the first time. Normally that payoff would be enough. Part of me wishes I had learnt to leave myself alone during the difficult times a lot sooner. Maybe Astrid would still be here if I had.

At the moment I seem to be doing an emotional stocktake. Tonight, I simply take stock of how much I miss Astrid. And if I'm honest, sometimes I feel like I am moving away from her. Every time I start to feel genuine fulfilment, I feel like I am disrespecting the gravity of our breakdown.

As weird as it sounds, it feels like I should keep this dialogue (and everything that's happening) a secret. It wouldn't seem proportional to talk about how happy I've felt at different stages. I don't want my happiness in the face of our relationship breakdown to be misinterpreted.

I guess everything I'm writing tonight is conceived from disappointment. I feel that way because I haven't had any contact with Astrid recently. I tried calling her today but she didn't answer. And she didn't return my call either. I miss that she notices me. I'm sad there is no avenue to notice her any more.

Mostly, I am concerned that opening my spiritual eyes will end up taking me away from Astrid. Perhaps I'm meant to accept that she is moving on without me. I'm scared that everything is proceeding the way it is meant to, and that means Astrid and I are finished.

Here I am again, sitting quietly in the middle of the night. I find myself looking up from these words.

Leaving yourself alone during difficult times isn't about constant happiness. Embracing the unknown isn't about that. It's not about getting what you want all of the time either. It's about acceptance. And that's not always about being happy.

Maybe it's about ending up exactly where you were headed. Maybe the unknown is about hitting precisely what you were aiming for. Perhaps the two realities I am facing at the moment are about accepting that Astrid and I are done. It's possible we are not meant to share what is coming next.

Tonight, embracing the unknown is about having no need to wipe the tears from my eyes. I'm going to bed.

Tuesday

I realise I haven't written much about how difficult things have been lately. But that doesn't mean everything in my life is peachy. Part of me thinks it would be a huge mistake to focus on the things that bring me down. I don't want this story to be exclusively about the struggles I've faced.

Astrid moved out because I allowed my life, and therefore our relationship, to be solely about the struggles we faced. Allowing that reality to be the central focus is also the reason I have left work. If I continue to relive all of that stuff, I will just be entering the same old negative cycle that caused the problems in the first place.

Not giving the difficult times a voice doesn't mean they are not present. I'm not referring to suppressing anything when I stipulate that. It's not about ignoring my thoughts or feelings. I won't push any of those things away. I am fully aware that if I suppress how I feel, I will not be able to move forward.

As I write that, I remember making a commitment to myself exactly two weeks ago. I deliberately told myself I would trigger a life-changing event with the lines of this story. I do not intend to waver from that commitment. As long as my hands write the words before me, I will consciously make this about moving forward.

I feel like I owe that to Jessica and Haylie. I certainly owe it to Astrid.

All of that was a long way of saying I have been quite down over the past couple of days. At least at different stages, I have felt bogged down by worry. The most difficult part about feeling like that isn't conceived from a lack of acceptance though. I do not expect constant happiness from my life. It's the manic nature of what's going on that's difficult to deal with. The ups and downs of the past three weeks have been quite harsh.

At any other time, I would be freaking out. But recognising the choice in what I tell myself is about leaving things alone. I don't need to add anything to the feeling of missing Astrid. It's not necessary to fortify the worry I have about my job prospects either. And there is no need to supress those things.

Seeing the choice in life is about observing things without reacting impulsively. But that doesn't mean I'm numb to what I am feeling. Quite the opposite is true. It's about acknowledging your feelings with honesty. It's about not adding meaningless stories to the feelings of loss.

Yet, even though I recognise everything I just said as the truth, I still feel a sense of grief sometimes. I still feel a deep sense of loss. I miss her so much. It's not entirely about the fact that we split up. The feeling of deep sadness is mainly about losing any hope there is for us. I might not feel desperate about what I'm going through all of the time. But I still feel heartbroken quite often.

As I commit to moving forward, I start to wonder if I'm meant to let go of the things that are stopping me from doing that. I wonder if I'm meant to release the things that leave me feeling heartbroken. And quite frankly, the idea of that is breaking my heart.

Wednesday

I can't stop thinking about a quote from the Tao philosophy…

'If you do not change direction, you may end up where you are heading.'

Lao Tzu is the founder of Taoism, and is said to be the inspiration behind the Tao Te Ching, a book about 'the way' of life, viewed from the perspective of the Tao philosophy. The Tao Te Ching has become one of the most translated texts in history, second only to the Bible. Interestingly, the very early stages of Christianity were also known as 'the way'.

I'm trying to find a way forward but I feel so confused. Doing an emotional stocktake is about identifying how I operate. Understanding the weight of negativity I created is driving me to take complete responsibility for how my life has unfolded to this point.

Once you accept that your problems come from your thoughts, the unknown is really the only path you can take as you look to change direction.

But I feel so confused because I can't see a way to bring Astrid with me as I create a new beginning. Every time I get close to fulfilment, I feel like I'm turning my back on our relationship.

Maybe it's time to act upon that reality. I can't afford to cling to something that doesn't exist. I will not find a way forward if I keep reliving the heartbreak I feel. Maybe it's time to fall backwards into the unknown. Perhaps I'm meant to trust the vulnerability that comes with that. I can't keep juggling the two different realities I referred to earlier. They seem to be stunting the process I'm unpacking here.

I guess it's time to act upon the finality of our relationship breakup.

CHAPTER FIVE

The Weird Things

'Every person walking the planet is worthy of something much bigger than the struggles they face.'

Thursday

What an exhausting day.

I wrote Astrid a goodbye letter this morning. The act of writing is really helping lately. I thought it would be good to stay in that pocket and express what I needed to in a letter. I basically apologised to her. I didn't ask for forgiveness though. I just told her that I understood why she left. And I said goodbye.

I have to admit, I have had a heavy heart all day. I've felt nervous and anxious from the moment I woke. It's been virtually impossible to sit still. I went to send the email to Astrid several times. But every time I finished re-reading it, I shot up from my seat and started pacing around. Despite that, I remained determined. I honestly thought sending the letter was something I needed to do. After the girls and I ate dinner, I sat at our kitchen bench and opened my laptop. I procrastinated a little more, but eventually I settled myself, took a deep breath and literally asked God to help me.

I was just about to press send on the email when Jess interrupted. She didn't say too much, but she looked quite emotional. After I asked what was wrong, she broke down and started crying. I hugged her and kept asking what had happened. She couldn't talk though. Her tears were too loud.

If I'm honest, I have to admit that part of me was relieved. Jess hasn't shown much emotion regarding Astrid moving out. She has refused to talk about it. I was starting to get worried she was harming her psyche by being too withdrawn. Although it was upsetting to see her to cry so deeply, I was also thankful because she was finally letting it all out.

By the time Jess had calmed down enough to talk, Haylie was with us. She is four years younger than Jess. The girls mean everything to each other. Whenever one of them is upset, the other is right there. Jess started talking about how much she missed Astrid. The mere mention of that set Haylie off. And then all three of us were crying together.

As I sit here writing, the girls are asleep next to me. We decided it was time for a midweek slumber party. We watched Disney movies and ate popcorn. I was happy to shut my laptop, and not think about the goodbye letter for the rest of the night. It wasn't a question of putting it off though. I walked away from it for different reasons.

Before our movie night started, I reassured the girls that everything would be okay. I told them time would help us heal. But Jess responded in a way that gave me a moment's pause. She said she wanted more than that. She was not prepared to wait for things to get better. I didn't know how to respond, so I asked what she wanted. Jess sat looking at me sharply without saying anything.

I didn't get it.

I looked at Haylie and said: 'What's going on?' Haylie looked at Jess and then said: 'Dad, you have to fight for her.' Jess responded by telling me that I can't give up on Astrid.

I impulsively slammed my laptop shut and pushed it away from us like it was about to detonate. As I write these words I feel so exhausted. I can't see anything clearly right now. I'm too confused to do anything definitive.

Perhaps I'm meant to fight for Astrid. Maybe I'm meant to go after her the way heartbreak wants love to chase it.

Friday

Let's talk about weird stuff.

After I dropped the kids at school I felt a little restless. I was weighing up if I should send Astrid the letter. I found myself staring out my front door. I was just standing there with my hands cupped behind my back. My eyes were focused, but looking at nothing in particular. I couldn't break my gaze for some reason. I wanted something different from the day. If I were to describe what I was looking for in one word, it would be 'anticipation'. I was completely still, looking for anticipation.

Once again, the silence grabbed my attention. I stood quietly considering why that was the case. In that precise moment, I wondered if I was putting off the inevitable. I thought it might be time to act. And then I felt heavy again. I didn't attach anything to the feeling though. I just stood still. As clear as something is heard from a backdrop of nothing, this came: 'Okay then, now what?'

But I heard no answer. I started to feel a little conspicuous so I broke my gaze and went to shut the front door. Almost immediately my phone buzzed. Tristan sent a text explaining we had to meet. He told me to come out his way tomorrow because he needed to tell me something. The tone of his message was slightly different to what he normally sent. He was more direct; almost like he was demanding I meet with him.

I replied, saying I was looking forward to it. As I typed the message in my phone, I noticed exactly the same feeling I have when I write in this forum. Noticing the similarity was strange to me. A scent of sharpness was in the air again. My awareness was heightened, and it was compelling.

Contemplating the unknown, embracing that reality, automatically makes you conscious.

I found myself looking outside again. I had no idea what Tristan wanted to talk about. But I knew it was important. From the backdrop of nothing, just a few moments ago, I asked myself what was next. And I guess Tristan answered in more ways than one. As I stood quietly thinking about seeing him tomorrow, he sent another message. That's when I knew for sure tomorrow was going to matter. I understood everything needed to be put on hold until then.

This is what the message read: 'Topic of conversation - Letting go of Astrid.'

Saturday

It's incredible that Tristan sent the message without knowing what Jess and Haylie said two nights ago. There's just no way those guys have talked. It has to be the Creative Force of the Universe at play. It has to be. I felt comforted and less exhausted today. Knowing everything was proceeding as it should be, left me with a feeling of peace. Not knowing what to expect didn't matter. It was enough to trust in the bigger picture. Trusting that reality left me with nothing else to worry about.

I have been taking stock a lot lately. As I drove to meet Tristan I couldn't understand why I hadn't checked in with him sooner. Quite frankly, we've always been there for each other throughout our adult lives. He's always steady and deliberate during the difficult times.

And he didn't waste any energy today. As soon as we met, he asked if I had figured out why Astrid and I broke up. I said a lot without answering him. Tristan was in no mood to muck around. He didn't interrupt while I was busy waffling. But when I finished talking, he said quite sharply 'you don't deserve her.'

He challenged me to start being honest with myself. He spoke about honouring love. A lot of what he said didn't mean that much to me. I asked what 'deserving someone' looked like. With a certain amount of tenacity, I challenged him to explain what honouring someone looked like on a practical level.

He replied without hesitation: 'The fact that you have to ask the question in the first place is an indication you don't deserve Astrid's love.'

Weirdly, I didn't feel insulted by what he was saying. I knew he was right. If I'm honest though, I have to admit that I wished his message was different. Initially, the anticipation of meeting him was much better than the reality. I guess the truth isn't always easy to hear. Especially when broken things need fixing.

Tristan emphasised that he wasn't trying to make me feel bad. His intent was not for me to beat myself up. I asked why it was so important that we met now.

He explained he knew how I operated. He knew instinctively I would be trying to unpack everything that had happened recently.

He told me he had a favour to ask. I automatically wanted to tell him about this dialogue. I wanted to spill the beans about everything. But for some reason I stopped myself from doing that. I asked what the favour was. And then I understood the timing of everything. From Tristan's answer, I got the message loud and clear.

He simply asked me to be gentle as I unpacked everything; that I remained steady until I found the answers. Tristan suggested that I not give up until I knew what it meant to honour love.

He finished by saying this: 'The answer isn't found in how amazing Astrid is. It's not about giving her something in order to win her back. And until you know what all of that means, don't do anything stupid.'

With that, he slapped me on the back and walked away. And lo and behold, I was left speechless.

Ripples *of* Stillness

Sunday

This is why I deleted the goodbye letter to Astrid…

Bryce rang me this morning. Much like the catch up with Tristan yesterday, he held the floor during our conversation. He explained that something had been playing on his mind, and he wanted to check in with me. He asked how things had been going lately.

I explained there was no action or intent with Astrid. I told him about the letter I wrote to her. I mentioned that I planned to send it but weird things kept stopping me. I thought he would ask for an explanation but he didn't. Instead, Bryce asked how I felt every time I considered saying goodbye to Astrid once and for all. I told him it felt like something I needed to do. And once again, his immediate response stopped me cold.

He said: 'That's not a feeling it's a simple thought process. You think it is something you have to do. But I asked you how it made you feel.'

And before I go on with this dialogue, I will emphasise that the truth is not difficult to find. If a person is earnestly willing to look, the truth will reveal itself in no uncertain terms.

Bryce remained silent, waiting for my response. He said gently: 'The answer shouldn't be that hard to find.'

I blurted out that I felt heavy every time I considered saying goodbye to Astrid. And then the avalanche of emotion started. I rambled about feeling desperate and incomplete. I talked about the feeling of regret I have been carrying around since she left. My mouth wouldn't stop. I really unloaded on him.

Although I was a little embarrassed when I finally calmed down, it also felt good to get everything off my chest. I was breathing quite fast once I finished. So I knew those feelings were waiting for a voice.

Bryce has a gentle disposition about him. Every time I start to get carried away, he seems to offer the complete opposite. He asked very quietly, why I would be contemplating letting go of any possibility of a fresh start with Astrid if doing so would leave me with those feelings. He said after hearing from me, he understood why he needed to call.

He challenged me not to give up on the things that worked. He reflected on our conversation at the beginning of the month. He reminded me about the struggle I created in my work. Bryce suggested that if I gave up on Astrid, I would simply be ignoring what I wanted for myself. He suggested that every person walking the planet was worthy of something much bigger than the struggles they faced.

At the end of our conversation, he challenged me to disregard the goodbye letter. He told me to take a risk with myself. He asked that I leave myself alone whenever I felt heavy. And then he said something before hanging up the phone that made my eyes sharpen.

He suggested it was time to start paying attention to the weird things.

CHAPTER SIX

The Certainty of the Unknown

'Starting with a clean slate isn't about falling backwards into the unknown. It takes intent. It requires action without expectation. Anything less would be about doubt and vanity.'

Monday

Jess hasn't been wearing makeup to school lately. On an average day, her eyes look like a nebula from outer space. Not recently though. Over the past month the girls and I have become a lot closer. We're engaging in meaningful, grounded conversations. We are sharing without waiting for a turn to talk. We're listening to each other without waiting for anything.

I've been assuming (in fact knowing) that Jess is becoming more comfortable within herself. It has been completely obvious she's finding her confidence. Without saying anything, I've felt both proud and connected to her. I've been walking around the house with a kind of confident strut. I recognised Jess' newfound comfort as an indication we're all doing well.

Sometimes confidence demands a voice.

Last night, as I was getting dinner ready, I casually mentioned to Jess that she looks beautiful without makeup. I tell her, whilst nodding my head slightly, that I've noticed. I crinkle my lips up, and whisper that I get it. I tell her that we're on a path of connection and closeness. I said I liked her new organic look.

This is what she said in return:

'Dad, what the hell are you talking about! I ran out of makeup ages ago and I'm waiting for you to buy me some more. I've already told you that. Twice!'

Then she walked to her bedroom. She was shaking her head and mumbling something about looking organic. Haylie sat at the kitchen bench gently laughing into the palm of her hand. All I could do was invoke a double chin, and wait for the moment to pass.

So I guess it's possible to transform your life with instinctive action, and at exactly the same time, be completely full of crap.

Point of interest: I stopped with the strut and spent time by myself for a little while.

Tuesday

So much of what I've always told myself is not true.

I almost convinced myself that moving forward meant starting again. But starting with a clean slate doesn't have to mean dropping what I want for my life. The evolution I'm going through doesn't have to be at the cost of the things I love the most. Once honesty is the motivation, I see that you can't grow emotionally if you throw love out with the trash.

A lot of what I have written lately has been about rocking my comfort zone. The past month has been about embracing the unknown. In fact, this entire dialogue came from wanting to change what I've always done. I have stipulated several times that I was going to make the events of the past month a life-changing event. And I hold true to that virtue.

But I can't afford to throw the baby out with the bathwater. There is no point in surrendering the things my heart truly wants. If I did that, the intent of this process would be entirely about deprivation. And I've been there before. I know what depriving myself looks like.

What I've always told myself can be a stubborn thing. In a lot of ways, my comfort zone wants to remain where it is. What I've done throughout my life comes from learned behaviour. It's programmed into the old grey matter. And it's been part of my behavioural DNA from the outset.

It's going to take conscious action to rock the comfort zone. I see now that part of what I'm going through could be a grind. If I don't bring actions to this process nothing will happen. Moving forward, I have to become my word in mind, body and spirit. I have to act upon my truth. It's not enough to simply listen to my heart. The only way to give my instincts any potency is to act on them.

Approaching each day looking at a blank page is a fitting metaphor to living without expectations.

But starting from nothing isn't about inaction. Rocking your comfort zone doesn't have to be entirely about dropping things. Starting with a clean slate doesn't have to be about falling backwards into the unknown screaming.

THE UNKNOWN

It takes intent. It requires action without expectation. Anything less would be about doubt and vanity.

And it's time to turn those things on their head.

Wednesday

I start today by lightly tapping the keyboard.

I still have no idea where half this stuff is coming from. Sometimes I feel like a member of the audience with this dialogue. That doesn't dilute the truth of what I'm writing though. I know, with the certainty of a sunrise, that what I am hearing is the truth. But I just can't explain yet how I know.

I guess what I've been putting on paper is simply inspired messages from within. I am writing without inhibitions, and therefore what I'm communicating is saturated with conviction. As I've already mentioned, I am writing without knowing what to say. I am taking part in free-association writing. My intention every day is to start from nothing. I write as if I'm the reader.

Hang on… I've said that before.

When I contemplate the idea of writing as if I'm the reader, I think about a well-known quote from Father Alfred D'Souza.

> *'Dance as though no one is watching you,*
> *Love as though you have never been hurt before,*
> *Sing as though no one can hear you,*
> *Live as though heaven is on earth.'*

I imagine Father D'Souza was completely connected to his authentic voice when he wrote that. I'm proud he lived in Australia. His quote reminds me of the idea that I'm writing without inhibitions. I don't always know what I'm going to say in this dialogue. I'm not always clear where some of it comes from. But I am having a conversation with myself, and I consciously choose to hold nothing back.

In committing to meet myself in this forum on a daily basis, I automatically leave my comfort zone. This dialogue is about letting go of what I have always told myself. It's about getting out of the way, and allowing a spontaneous message to flow onto the page. The lines of this story are about waking from my slumber. I am waking up to the truth of my life. I'm starting to see the stillness that sits beneath the preoccupations of doubt and worry.

I am becoming as certain as a sunrise.

Thursday

I touch my tattoos for some reason. It has me thinking about the depths of love. So much of the past month has been about how much I miss Astrid. As weird as it might sound, the thing I miss the most is watching her sleep. She always cuddles this white fluffy little teddy bear that's wearing a bright red bowtie. Astrid's a German scientist, with a serious job. She's an intelligent mature woman. And yet most nights, she falls asleep snuggled up to this little teddy bear. I miss seeing that.

The past month has felt like a mountain. So much has happened in a short time. On my best day I'm able to keep out of the way. In doing so, I trust the Creative Force of the Universe. The past week has been an appropriate illustration of that. I was set to do something really stupid. Sending a letter to Astrid, relinquishing all hope for us, would have been a huge mistake. I am compelled to trust in the Creative Force of the Universe after everything that's happened lately. Too much has unfolded to be blind to the collective message from everyone.

I guess it all started by acknowledging that I am dealing with two realities. One is quite spiritual and involves waking to something more than my doubts. The other is about missing Astrid so often. I almost convinced myself that I had to drop the latter in order to continue with the former. It was only through sharing with others that I was able to see beyond that line of thinking.

Thank God for the people in my life.

Embracing the unknown isn't about smothering the past. I don't have to turn my back on where I've come from. Once I acknowledge and validate the past, I can accept the unknown without any baggage. I don't have to give up on what works in order to move forward. I can simply bring that stuff with me as I look for a new beginning.

With that philosophy in mind, I stepped up today. I did something for my own sake. I wrote a different letter to Astrid. I apologised for leaving her behind. It was a brief message explaining that I've decided to call myself out. I told her I would earn what happened to us. But most importantly, I told Astrid I would wait for her. I said I would wait for as long as she needed. I wrote without reservation this time. I finally got to say that she was the love of my life. I explained that no matter what happened in the future, everything was going to be okay. I told her the scent of our relationship would always be with me.

And I sent the email without hesitation. I was not nervous about the outcome because I wasn't attached to one. Once again, she didn't reply. But I see now that it doesn't really matter. At least she knows how I feel. At least I was honest with myself. I got to tell her that I would wait.

Thank God for the people in my life.

Friday

Victor Hugo (author of *Les Misérables*) wrote:

> *'To love another person is to see the face of God.'*

I am just so thankful for the people in my life. I've had so much love and support over the past month. It has been a beacon of light. The relationship I share with others is the reason I can see through the darkness.

Obviously, the darkest times are when I miss Astrid. It seems the happier I get, the more I wish she were home to share it. Every day, I'm flanked by surprise of how abruptly our relationship ended. When she first left I'd wake up every morning and (before I'd come to my senses) feel relieved for a couple of seconds because I thought the whole ordeal was just a bad dream, almost like a warning.

At least I'm not starting each day with disappointment any more. Things are getting easier. When I consider that, I automatically picture the people in my life. Mum has called me every day over the past month. Somehow she has done it without being intrusive. Her devotion is constant. Her support is unwavering but flexible. Her words are soft yet confronting.

Nic has been a steady influence as well. She has become my ambassador of fun and spontaneity. Her instincts are brilliant. Her energy is infectious. It's difficult to wallow in self-pity when Nicola is around. My brother Jamie reminds me of the importance of family bonds. Who he is, shows me who I want to be for others. My father has taught me about the significance of taking responsibility. He constantly shows me the creative force of a person's word. Without his influence, I'm not sure I could communicate so honestly in this context.

I can't explain why, but Bryce always seems to make contact around the same time Tristan does. They don't have much to do with each other. I'm certain they don't keep in regular contact. And yet, they always show up at the same time. They always seem to have the same message. Bryce sent me one today.

Just before I received it, I was contemplating the connection people shared. I was walking through a park thinking about how important relationships were. As I thought about that, my phone buzzed. Quite often, a friendship is fortified by instinct alone. Without any explanation, Bryce sent me this short message:

> 'We are not measured by the length of our doubts. We find ourselves through the things we share.'

After reading it, my awareness heightened. It made my eyes shine. I couldn't help but think about Jessica and Haylie. I love them so much. Often, all I need to do is trust that.

I say what I'm about to after a long pause of staring at nothing in particular. It's difficult for me to put into words how much Jess and Haylie mean to me.

I'll simply let my fingers explain it.

Imagine all of us actually do have a guardian angel. Then picture that one day my guardian angel comes across a genie in a bottle. As everyone knows, the story dictates that he gets three wishes. Imagine my guardian angel uses his first wish to wake me from my slumber. The genie, recognising his audience, dispenses with the theatrics and says: 'Okay then, now what?'

With quiet confidence, the angel wishes I be granted all the fulfilment the world has to offer. He wishes that my life be saturated with love and understanding. With light and warmth. He requests that I be granted direction, substance and strength. That even in my darkest moments, I stay connected to the miracles of gratitude.

The genie replies sharply: 'That's impossible. You only have two wishes left. You know I'm governed by this universal truth. I can't achieve all of that in only two wishes.'

With unwavering trust, the angel looks to the stars and says very gently: 'That you would replace the source of your power with doubt...'

Not wanting to be outdone, the genie starts to create from nothing. He rattles faith with a click of his fingers. At that precise moment, from the other side of heaven, a whiff swirls.

Having nothing more to say to each other, the two entities part ways without a second glance. They were smiling the same smile. In that cosmic-moment, Jessica and Haylie were sent as my children.

They are my last two wishes. Sent from the angels of heaven.

PART TWO

September

The Light of Relationships

CHAPTER SEVEN

The Descent of Doubt

*'It's the conviction of certainty that sustains a relationship.
It's a form of certainty that is devoid of arrogance.
It's a gentle, supplicating type of conviction.'*

Saturday 1 September

It's time to square off with myself.

I'm going to call myself out. It was not necessarily my intention, but last month I spoke about heartbreak quite a bit. I feel less heartbroken lately. Retrospectively, I understand my relief comes from being honest with myself. Communicating without inhibition allows me to let go of things I was once protective of.

This is where I let go of the things I have been clinging to. I am motivated for change. From the very outset, I chose to take on what keeps happening in my intimate relationships. Well, it's time to meet that reality with intent.

So much of what I have done in the past no longer serves me. I don't want the life I once had any more. I see now that stepping into the unknown isn't about being blind or uncertain. There's no need to let go of everything that got me to this point. Quite the opposite is true. Embracing the unknown is about accepting every aspect of the past. It comes from acknowledging the footprints of your life without wanting to retrace your steps.

I no longer feel protective about my past. It's a beautiful feeling to let go of that reality. Once you leave the past where it belongs everything becomes bright and so much cleaner. You can move forward without any pollution clouding the way. I am reminded that the lines of this story are about growth. I am here for the purposes of evolution. I find myself committed to this process so that I can change the events of my life. I'm here to create a new beginning.

What I've done in the past isn't about right or wrong though.

I do not view my life before now as bad. Looking for growth isn't about what was wrong with me. If I spend time belittling myself, then I am just entering another self-defeating cycle. Squaring off with myself is about breaking self-defeating cycles of behaviour. Calling myself out is about being honest.

This process is about waking up to my life. I give myself permission to hold nothing back because no one else is listening. I have nothing to lose here. This dialogue is about finding my highest reality. On my best day, I use my authentic voice to achieve that.

It's time to strip back the excuses:

- Here is where I will own my distractions.
- Now is when I stand up.

The things that prevented me from reaching my highest reality were created from within. They were not wrong; it's more precise to say they were small. The reality I created for myself was not bad; it's just that parts of it were dark. And it's time to address that softly.

What I am going to do next isn't solely about my own personal growth. It's time to unpack what keeps happening with my intimate relationships for the sake of the very thing I am putting on the line - my relationships with others.

Sunday

It's Father's Day.

Often, when I am struggling to make sense of something, I picture what I would tell Jess and Haylie. Whenever I am deeply lost I just put on my parental hat. Being Jess and Haylie's father has always made perfect sense to me. It just feels right. Being their Dad is part of my heart's work. I have paid tribute to them several times already, and that's fitting because of how much they mean to me.

However, I'm mindful not to talk about them too often. I don't want the potency of the message to be thinned by overstating how I feel. One of the great things about what we share is that it isn't measured by extremes any more. What we have together is easy.

It's the conviction of certainty that sustains our relationship. However, it's a form of certainty that is devoid of arrogance. It's a gentle, supplicating type of conviction. Which is to say, I am always looking into the verbs of my parenting. I'm more than willing to learn as a father. I welcome parental challenges, because I see them as opportunities for growth. There is no doubt in the parental question I ask of myself though. I can look at ways to evolve without second guessing anything.

What I have with Jess and Haylie serves as an example. We can disagree or argue without questioning how we feel about each other. There can be times of physical and emotional distance without any of us having feelings of loneliness. There are no questions of doubt in our relationship. What we have is clean. It has always been one big unconditional play of love.

I don't bring up Jess and Haylie again in order to overstate what they mean to me. I am not simply paying homage to that. The point I'm making goes much deeper than words of appreciation.

I am talking about the connection we share because it shows what a relationship can be. I understand, and in fact welcome, that there is a big difference between loving someone, and being in love. I'm not dismissing that.

I don't think it's a simple case of acknowledging the depths of love though. It's more about the faith we have in each other. It's the conviction of certainty that sustains what we share.

In truth, there's no Father's Day gift the kids could offer that would be greater than what has already been given. But that doesn't have to mean something happened to us. It's not a question of being lucky or chosen somehow. Our relationship is a cultivation of generosity, love and gratitude. The process of us starts with acting upon how we feel.

And it's time to look up from that reality and see what else is out there. It's time to honour what was given, by sharing it with others.

I'm referring to a possibility here.

If I am certain about being a parent, then it has to be possible to become certain about being a partner. I can go from experiencing relationship breakups, to having relationship breakthroughs. If I trust the love I have for my kids, then I can trust it with others as well.

The reason is simple.

'Love does not discriminate'

Monday

When I refer to a future relationship with someone special, I will be referring to a future with Astrid.

Nic asked me recently if I'm prepared for the possibility that Astrid and I will not get back together. She suggested I consider what would happen, so I'm emotionally ready if it does. I completely understand why Nic is asking me to polish the apple here. There will be a very loud thud if Astrid tells me there is no chance for us. The music will stop instantly if all hope is removed. However, I consciously choose not to give any energy to that possibility.

I'm not talking about sticking my head in the sand and pretending it will never happen. I just choose not to smother any hope for us until it is evident I have to. At the moment that's hard to accept because I haven't heard from Astrid in a while. Sometimes the doubt I feel about the lack of contact between us is pretty loud. But I'm learning to leave myself alone during the times of doubt.

I have to believe that what I am going through is bigger than the noise of doubt. I need to trust the current momentum of my life. And I choose to believe that my broader purpose involves Astrid. If she decides to move on, then I will deal with that when it happens. But my heart tells me to hold on. It's the silence beyond the reality of doubt that brings me comfort. When I'm able to trust that, I genuinely feel I should hold on to hope for us.

I think this dialogue is about waking up. I'm pretty sure it's about activating my highest reality. And if all of that is true, it will be for her.

Tuesday

And the penny drops. Astrid is away with work. That's why I haven't heard from her recently. She sent me an email last night explaining she is in the Pilbara. I should have known; I don't know why I didn't think of that. As an environmental scientist, she is always flying off to remote areas to do her work. When the seasons are behaving themselves, she is normally away for at least a week each month.

She pointed out a couple of things in her email. But before I address them, I need to emphasise the importance of leaving things alone. Sometimes certain situations need room to breathe. Especially when doubt is the baseline emotion. I just assumed Astrid was ignoring me. I thought she didn't want to talk. But as it turns out, there was a logical reason she hadn't responded.

She apologised for the lack of contact after explaining that she doesn't have very good reception where she is based. Apparently, it's been quite difficult to check emails. She also thanked me for the letter I sent five days ago. She titled her response 'Phew!'

That made me laugh and quiver at the same time for some reason.

Astrid said it was flattering to read how much she meant to me. She thought any girl would enjoy hearing such a heartfelt message. But at the same time, she said she couldn't ask me to wait for her. She thought that would be unfair on both of us. She was too unsure about what the future held.

She said she would understand if I needed to move on. In fact, I was encouraged to do so if getting a definitive answer, one way or another, would bring me peace.

Her email also addressed just how often I was caught up in the struggles of my work. She gently explained that our connection was lost in the constant rumination of my life. She needed something more from love. She referred to the darkness that entered our home because of the struggles we faced.

And then, in a very heartfelt way, she apologised for dismantling the devotion of us.

THE LIGHT *of* RELATIONSHIPS

She also acknowledged that part of her wants to believe I've changed. But then she said something that reminded me she is a German scientist with a very analytical way of looking at the world. She doesn't believe a person can change his or her mind because of a simple realisation. She sees that as flimsy and unsustainable.

I love her brain. She's such a smart cookie.

Astrid needs action, not just words. I see now that it's going to take showing her who I am. Broad sweeping platitudes are not going to cut it as we move forward. I'm going to need actions to find her again. And I'm totally up for it.

I've never been more certain of my love for a woman. I was not hurt by what she wrote either. Three days ago I said it was time to call myself out. And I guess Astrid just did that in more ways than one. I responded to her briefly. I explained I would show her that it's possible for one simple realisation to change everything.

I said it was the only thing that ever has.

Wednesday

I struggle to put into words just how often I was stuck in my head. So much of my life depended on struggling. There was a palpable staleness in our home. The energy of life was musty and thin. A descent of doubt had infiltrated everything. It's no wonder my life came to a grinding halt. The lack of action was so dark. What was happening required something drastic.

A person listening to this story would not be able to conceive just how often I sat around watching TV, or zoning out to my so-called smart phone. I missed so much of my life because I was busy checking out Facebook or looking for trending hashtags. I was constantly flicking through my life. I would bounce from one mind-numbing distraction to another. I justified all of it by thinking it was relaxing.

The inaction of life became my comfort. And a break from that reality normally involved spending money. Getting out of the house meant buying something shiny. My fleeting happiness could be found in a flat-pack or in something new to play with. A productive day was measured by how exhausted I was at the end of it. Socialising involved small talk and politely agreeing with everyone. I was convinced all of that stuff mattered. It didn't even occur to me to question it.

It was the routine of my life that made everything tight.

But the stuff I was clinging to seems trite to me now. As I sit here writing these words, I see no need to choke my life. The values that I hold, the picture I see, does not require a strong grip. There is no need to cling to routine in order to feel safe. The life I see for myself, my highest reality, is free from the tension of doubt and rumination.

In many ways, moving forward is about leaving certain things alone. The descent of doubt I felt was kept alive with action. I was convinced the struggle I faced was justified. Trusting there was no other way to operate validated everything. My experience was limited to trusting the self-defeating cycle I had created for myself.

The Light *of* Relationships

It's a paradox in many respects.

Perhaps the best thing I can do is to leave things alone. I just look past what I've always told myself. Self-defeating thoughts of doubt become less potent after you step back from them. Rather than acting impulsively, you simply notice them.

When I leave doubt alone I feel less confused. And then I see something infinitely larger than the routine of safety I was clinging to. Beyond the lifeboat of structure that I was hiding in, there is a light of possibility that stretches past the horizon. It is a light that cannot be measured.

And I don't remember seeing anything like that in a hashtag.

Thursday

Life is bigger than the doubts we create. It's time to own my behaviour. Realising that I create my reality means I want to be gentle. When I think about going easy on myself, I see the magnitude of self-imposed strain I lived with. I was completely measured by extremes. I had so many rules, or quirky superstitions that directed my behaviour.

There is a popular song that's out at the moment, which relates to what I'm talking about. *Some Nights* by the band Fun could be an appropriate soundtrack to my life lately. There's a line in the chorus that hits the mark:

> *'That's alright, I found a martyr in my bed tonight;*
> *stops my bones from wondering just who I am'*

The song is about waking up to your place in life. It's about finally standing up and taking complete responsibility for where you find yourself. For me, it speaks to the self-defeating martyr I had created in order to feel safe. I had heaps of things in place to stop me wondering who I am. I created so many quirky rules so I didn't have to look at my life. I had surrendered to the fiction of my internal dialogue. All of the rules and superstitions were an extension of living in my head.

The noise of my thoughts was deafening.

As I look to own my behaviour, I feel it's appropriate to map out exactly how exhausting I made things. These are merely some of the rules I had in place. Here is precisely why I call what was happening 'the struggle'.

- Wear only Nike shoes.
- Only burn jasmine incense.
- Only clean on certain days.
- Hoard money because there's never enough.
- Certain clothing for sporting activities and don't ever change that rule.
- Pretend you don't like animals.
- Never be barefoot.
- Wear only those socks.

- Remain philosophical at all costs.
- Cut your hair the same way every time.
- Worry, struggle, withdraw.
- Isolation is respite.
- The system is all there is.

Bloody hell, pull up dude!

It is almost exhausting writing all of that. What a way to live. I put so much pressure on myself. All of that was in my head constantly. The noise never stopped. Those are just some of the rules that dominated and crowded my life. It was all part of my system for survival. It was the metaphorical lifeboat I was clinging to.

I don't regret or dislike that side of me though. Mostly, I find it quite funny. But I am also cautious to look back on it with soft eyes. I am but a sum total of my experiences. Consequently, I address where I've come from with gratitude and understanding. I do not view that stuff as wrong. The fictional rules I had in place are not bad. It's just that they no longer serve a purpose.

I see a new picture now. I choose to look up from the reality that once was, and see a fresh start. I am free to write a new story coming from nothing. I start by replacing the system of self-imposed rules with something much simpler - the act of creation.

Friday

The Struggle.

When I look back on it, I don't know whether to laugh or slap my forehead. It's therapeutic to address old patterns of behaviour. It's not a question of being a martyr and beating myself up. I'm not here to act like Eeyore. It's more about being honest with myself. The strength behind the honesty comes from a willingness to be vulnerable.

Writing really helps with that. I understand that the formal act of writing every day is helping me identify who I am and where I've come from. Naming old patterns of behaviour helps objectify them. Giving the struggles I faced a title, helps separate me from the potency of it. It becomes something I do, rather than something I am.

I started at the beginning of the month on a quest to understand personal intimate relationships better. Surprisingly, it seems in order to do that honestly I'm compelled to call myself out first. Understanding what makes a relationship work seems to be about understanding what I bring to it. I don't see how I can be successful in a relationship if I go into it blindly. If I don't know who I am, then I can't offer that to someone else.

Consequently here I am, rag-dolling who I am.

In some ways, it's easy to see why Astrid and I fell apart. I was flippant and unengaged with her. Astrid ignored those things for the sake of our love. But I didn't offer her anything else. I guess she stayed because of our potential, and ended up leaving because of the reality she faced.

She was a passenger in the drama of my life. Our relationship breakdown was simply collateral damage of the dramas I created. In truth, I didn't care about her enough. I only cared about our relationship because the handbook said I should. It was nothing more than a theory. But my actions didn't mirror the theory of our relationship.

I guess Tristan was right. I don't deserve Astrid's love. Or at least, my actions during our relationship were not worthy of her. Everything I've unpacked over the past week has been about recognising what I brought to our relationship. An intimate relationship can serve as a mirror of how people treat themselves.

I created a path of destruction so that I could hide from the potential of my life. I was systematically tearing apart my relationship with Astrid because acting small was easier than owning my place in the world. Truth be told, I treated Astrid exactly the same way I was treating myself. I didn't care about my own growth, so how could I care about hers?

And starting right now, all of that changes. I'll replace what was once small with the vulnerability of trusting that I am worthy of something bigger. I will activate the responsibility of my life by turning to the love that created it.

CHAPTER EIGHT

What Works

'Action might not always bring you fulfilment but its opposite certainly won't. Inaction simply creates inaction.'

THE LIGHT *of* RELATIONSHIPS

Saturday

Listen!

I'm thankful this conversation is a one-way mirror. Because quite often I have no idea what I'm saying. I still don't know where half of this stuff is coming from.

But let me just say, sometimes it's a huge rush. I've never felt anything like it before. I get this weird surge of energy in the centre of my chest when I write. Things just seem to slip away when I'm here. There's a type of awareness that's quite hard to pinpoint. In addition to all of that, I have absolutely no idea where this is taking me. For some reason, I am reluctant to even question it.

From the very beginning of this story I committed to changing my life for the better. Originally, I opened a conversation with myself because I didn't know what else to do. I no longer wanted to sit around constantly worrying and doubting everything. Initially, this was about occupying myself.

But I'm starting to get the sense there's something much bigger at play. And although I have no idea what any of that means, I feel compelled to just go with it. Maybe it's simply a question of finding what works for someone. Maybe it's about finding fulfilment. I'm not entirely sure.

I guess it's the x-factor.

I am reminded of how a person conveys a message. Dr Albert Mehrabian came up with the theory that 55 per cent of our communication is body language. Only 7 per cent of communication is conveyed through words. The other 38 per cent is about how we say things. Sometimes I wish I could tap into the 55 per cent body language part of my communication skills to explain what's happening. Maybe I could flap my arms and dance the funky chicken to understand what's going on here.

Sunday

It actually feels right to acknowledge some of the things that have been working for me lately. So much of my life is different now. I almost don't recognise the person I see in the mirror any more. And most of the time, that's a good thing.

When I contemplate the gravity of change that has swept through my world, I can't help but notice how busy I've been. I no longer sit around waiting for things to happen. In fact, I'm far busier now than when I worked full time. My life, each day in each week, is full of purpose and action.

One thing that works well for me at the moment is exercise. I have exercised one way or another my entire adult life. In the past, I normally went to the gym three times a week. I was motivated to keep active because I wanted a healthy body. I didn't want to struggle with different physical ailments. But in all honesty, I was mainly exercising because of vanity.

My workouts were a perfect representation of the rest of my life. They were sloppy and apathetic. I would punch out different drills as quick as I could. And normally, I would hightail it out of the gym so fast you would have thought getting out of there was part of the workout. Ironically, on the days I exercised, I would feel nothing but dread. I would wake up, realise it was a gym day, roll my eyes and groan into my pillow.

I guess the obvious question is why do it if I hated it so much. Firstly, that's exactly how vain I was. Secondly, the contradiction was all part of the struggle. Feeling dread about having to exercise but still doing it was all part of living in my head.

But now I keep active for different reasons. I exercise every day to focus my mind and body. I use the time in the gym to silence the outer world and quieten my thoughts. Attempting to detach from your thoughts by simply wishing they would go away would be like trying to stop a tidal wave by pointing your elbows at it.

Detaching from your thoughts sometimes requires the focus and intent of action. A very easy way in which to silence your inner-world is by giving your complete attention to what you are doing. And that's entirely what keeping active is about for me now. My workouts are no longer sloppy and apathetic. They are about being mindful of the moment. My focus is not on the outcome. I'm not training for an athletic body. I no longer exercise out of obligation either. Exercising has stopped being about rules.

Of course I still want to look after my body. But that has become a natural by-product rather than the point. I pay attention to what my body needs and how it feels. I work on my concentration. I exercise as a means to tune in, rather than a way to tune out. Engaging in physical activity has become a profound way to practise mindfulness.

Being mindful of the moment is the protein-hit to having peace of mind.

I would never have guessed that peace of mind came from engagement. Sitting around waiting for things to happen achieves nothing. All you get from sitting around is the experience of sitting around. All you get from waiting is the experience of waiting.

The stillness of choice awaits our engagement.

Monday

I really appreciate the fact that what I am going through is an organic experience. I'm not pinning everything on wonderment and hope. I am bringing action to the idea of living out my highest reality. Paying attention to what matters is about acting on instinct.

However, bringing action to your life isn't about being incredibly busy all of the time. That reality is about avoidance and oblivion. Engaging in life has nothing to do with being unconscious. Going after fulfilment sometimes requires focused contemplation.

When acknowledging the things that are working, I have to mention meditation. In fact, I have no idea why I haven't brought it up sooner. Meditation could be the single most important exercise I'm doing in order to wake from my slumber.

Ever since I left work, I have been meditating every day. As soon as I wake up, I meditate for at least 10 minutes. I have also been meditating straight after physical exercise. Once finished, I sit quietly and regulate my breathing. I slow everything down with considered concentration.

In fact, I'm meditating whenever my instincts call on me to do so. Initially, it was about getting away from myself. The heartbreak I felt when Astrid left was too great. Meditation gave me a break from the feeling of despair. I didn't find it boring because it separated me from the deafening noise of my doubts.

Meditation started as a way to detach from my thoughts. It was a welcome break from the nonstop noise in my head. However, it has become something much bigger, and infinitely deeper than a tool for respite. The act of meditating regularly is showing me something I would have never imagined possible.

That the light of the horizon is also found within.

Tuesday

The importance of engaging in meaningful conversation cannot be understated. There is definitely room in this dialogue to acknowledge the importance of the company you keep. Often, if you want to know what sort of life you're leading, then simply pay attention to the conversations you have.

This ongoing dialogue is an appropriate example of the power of a person's word. The momentum of your life can be sustained by what you are telling yourself and how you are sharing that with others. We are all telling a story. The accent and influence of your story can be reflected in the company you keep.

As I acknowledge that, I look up for a moment.

I can't help but think about just how stressful my job was in the end. There were still plenty of things that made the job worthwhile. I still had plenty of reasons to be thankful. But at the same time, the pressures were immense in the end. They broke me. Or more precisely, the pressure I faced broke the status quo.

When I think about the importance of the company you keep, I remember just how stressful I found my job. Doing it well was so important to me. I wanted vocational success at any cost. Or so I thought. The stress infiltrated almost every other part of my life. It seems Jess and Haylie were the only people who had immunity from the deprivation.

Looking back on the whole thing reminds me of how easily the intent for your life can influence how it's played out. And as I write that, I realise something quite cool. I have not had many small conversations recently. I have engaged in a lot of meaningful conversations with others.

And today was no exception.

Nic randomly showed up demanding we go out. Her spontaneity and passion is infectious. But that does not mean she is without depth. Nicola has a considered and grounded disposition that not enough people notice. Today she threw me into her car and started driving around without a destination in mind.

We ended up at the first restaurant we came across. We shared good food, nice wine and great conversations.

To begin with, it seemed like a run-of-the-mill sort of catch up. But it didn't take long for Nic to ask how I was going. She questioned if I was paying attention to the process before me. I thought about this dialogue, and all the other things that have been working lately.

Nic listened to my broad sweeping statements about nothing in particular for as long as she could. But eventually she interrupted, and declared it was time for me to stop mucking around with life. She used a term that struck a chord. She said it was time 'to remain heavy on the earth.' Nic said everything that had happened recently led me to this point. And now it was time for action.

That made me burst. I told her everything about this dialogue and the weird things that had been going on. I spilled the beans about what happened on the ninth of August. I talked about detaching from my thoughts. I let it all out. I couldn't stop either. I tried to a couple of times but my mouth wouldn't shut up. By the time I had finished, I was concerned the conversation had become a verbal mugging. I sat quietly, feeling a little embarrassed. Nic simply looked up at the sky and said two words very loudly.

'Thank God!'

And then she hugged my face for a little bit too long.

Wednesday

Action might not always bring fulfilment, but its opposite certainly won't. Inaction simply creates inaction.

Engaging in life can be the spark to creating fulfilment. However, it's not about keeping busy so that you can avoid your life. That reality is totally about suppression. I bring verbs to my world in order to pay attention.

In many ways, paying attention to what matters comes from letting go of the stranglehold you have on your hopes and dreams. But it's not about giving up on those things. It comes from understanding that without engagement, your hopes and dreams lay dormant.

For so long, I sat around waiting for my hopes and dreams to prove something to me. The prosperity I pictured was nothing more than a metaphoric table at a casino. The only thing I brought to the creation of my fulfilment was the rigid clenched fist of hoping things would turn out well. The whole thing was a crapshoot.

There was no responsibility in it. Expectations disappear when you take responsibility for who you are and how you got here. Understanding that reality is also why I'm able to call myself out without getting depressed. What I've done, and where I'm going has nothing to do with hoping things will work out in the end. When I own my behaviour my attention sharpens.

Act on what works and you'll bring intent to your life. When you stop waiting and get busy with your instincts something weird happens. Life becomes what you've always hoped and dreamed it would.

Thursday

Okay I'm starting to get a little bored.

I need to move on. But before I do, I should clarify something. Identifying what works is about reaching fulfilment. And it's very much a moving target. It's a subjective thing, and it should remain that way. What works for me might not necessarily suit everyone.

When I talk about truth, I am simply referring to my truth. Not The Truth. When I refer to finding fulfilment, I don't think it's a case of one-size-fits-all. I can only find what works for me based on the life I've lived. Ultimately, I can't assume to speak for others, because I have not walked in their shoes.

That's not to dismiss the idea of empathy. The ability to empathise is a comforting pillow we all need. Being empathic can be like an emotional massage. Sometimes it's the only thing that keeps people close. However, that doesn't mean you can speak for everyone without his or her consent.

I think about my job again. Just because I found it toxic before taking a break, doesn't mean others should view it the same way. My point of view about the job is unique to my experience. It's also subjective. Further to that, the stress I felt in the end doesn't negate all the amazing experiences I had. The fulfilment I once got from the job was not an illusion. I just grew out of it.

The whole idea of identifying what works is about finding fulfilment. Both of those things are moving targets.

And there's almost no scenario where that is not true. I said I couldn't speak for everyone. But in truth, I can't even speak for some of my closest friends. To use just one example, I think about Tristan. He is completely devoted to his Christian faith. He says he knows no deeper truth than the one found in Jesus Christ. Some of the things I'm saying here would not suit his higher purpose. But that doesn't mean what works for me is invalid. Nor for that matter, is Tristan's faith.

Finding fulfilment is relative to the individual. Like most things in life, it's not about invalidating one point of view in order to reinforce another. When I refer to finding fulfilment in things such as writing, exercise and meditation, I'm simply talking about what works for me.

Perhaps there is no greater gift someone could give himself or herself than to eat cake and take a break from exercise. From a certain point of view, writing could be what brings someone down. On some levels, I even think it could be possible to meditate too often. Perhaps too much meditation could make someone withdraw from the world.

What I'm referring to isn't just about a person's right to choose either. It goes much deeper than a question of free will. The relative nature of finding what works is about growth. If growth were set in stone it wouldn't be what we call it. Bringing action into your world is about waking up to the potential for your life.

And it has absolutely nothing to do with being right.

CHAPTER NINE

New Beginnings

'New beginnings don't always require a cataclysmic shift of consciousness. Not always. Sometimes the smallest thing can make the biggest difference.'

THE LIGHT *of* RELATIONSHIPS

Friday

Well shave my face and pretend I'm ready!

I was wandering around the house slightly bored today. I didn't know where to put myself. For a brief moment, I questioned the point of what's been going on lately. I felt inquisitive rather than confused though. As always, I thought it would be a good idea to engage in the day. Just as I was about to grab my car keys and go for a drive there was a knock at the door. For some reason, I assumed it was a deliveryman or a door-to-door charity guy. I reached for my wallet as I opened the door. And then my heart skipped a beat out of nervousness.

It was Astrid. She stood in the doorway smiling at me. It took me a few seconds to settle, and notice that she was holding a picnic basket. It took even longer to notice I was just standing there with a dumb look on my face. Eventually, she just rolled her eyes and said: 'Calm down Simon, it's just a picnic. Hurry up and get your stuff.'

As it turns out, she just got back from working away. She had a few days off and thought we could both use an insignificant day together. We went to Kings Park and had exactly that. It was one of the most relaxing times we've had. We didn't really talk about anything too heavy. Without acknowledging it, we both kind of stayed in the moment and relaxed into things.

Astrid packed an impressive picnic. She laid out lots of different food. All of it looked amazing. We ate well and enjoyed pleasant conversation. Mostly, we simply watched as the beautiful spring weather of Perth passed us by.

Before long, Astrid asked how work was going. From her question, I suddenly realised just how rarely we've spoken lately. I had neglected to tell her I left work when she moved out. She wasn't surprised to find out though. She thought I desperately needed a break. She asked when I would be going back. But I couldn't be honest and answer at the same time.

I said everything on the work-front remained unclear. Astrid nervously scratched the back of her hand as she acknowledged how tough that must be to deal with. She looked away with strain on her face. I knew she would have been thinking about how often I revelled in the drama of my work. As she stared off into the distance, I saw her remembering just how lonely we both were in the end.

And in a blink, I realised how heartbroken she must have felt for so long. Quite frankly, my feeling of rock bottom only started recently. But the music stopped for Astrid ages ago. She lost me, before her very eyes, over months of desperation and anguish. And I could see the sadness in her face as she sat on the picnic rug remembering.

Without thinking I said: 'Truth is, you loved me enough to come and get me from the darkness. And I'm deeply sorry I left you there.'

She gently gulped as she tried to fight something back. A tear started to well in her eyes as she looked down at her lap. The insignificance of the day was slipping away quickly. I didn't want that to happen. I impulsively nudged her sideways. But I accidently pushed her hand onto a piece of cake. She laughed gently, and smeared the rest of it on my face.

The whole thing felt new somehow.

THE LIGHT *of* RELATIONSHIPS

Saturday

I can't believe Astrid showed up like that. I felt like a little kid on Christmas morning after waking today. It was the first time in a while that I woke because of genuine excitement. However, I want to be clear with myself. I don't feel that way because of a misplaced sense of hope that Astrid and I will get back together. Weirdly, the opposite is closer to the truth.

No matter what the future holds, I understand that what we once shared is finished. After yesterday, I see now that what we are dealing with is in fact a relationship breakup. The truth is, we are not simply going through a temporary separation. What we had was finite and it's done.

And Astrid completely agrees. After she dropped me home, I was just about to get out of her car. I had one foot on the driveway. Holding the door open, I looked back at her and said: 'It's finished isn't it?' She made a slight huffing sound as she looked at me. We both nodded silently.

As I write that, I feel a little sad.

But in truth, what we had finished at 5:35pm, Saturday the 28th of July. That was precisely when Astrid moved out. I remember marking the time and date as she left. Even back then, I knew it was going to matter. As I reflect on it, I understand there's no going back. Even if I could erase the past I would choose not to.

But that does not smother hope for the two of us. Acknowledging that what we had is gone can be an amazing gift. We get to start afresh. We have an opportunity to start again as friends, without the baggage of expectations. Astrid seemed like a different person yesterday. Of course she remained familiar but there was an emotional scent of freshness about her. I found myself looking at her through new eyes. The excitement I felt this morning came from understanding that Astrid and I now have a blank page in front of us.

And if we pay attention as we move forward, we can write a new story. If we use maturity and purpose, we just might find a new beginning. All of that doesn't necessarily mean we will end up back together. But if we add conscious intent, we can create something bigger than the finality that eventually ended us. Moving forward can be about a possibility that is devoid of expectations. We can look at each other with new eyes. And no matter what happens that's a gift.

THE LIGHT *of* RELATIONSHIPS

Sunday

I couldn't stop thinking about the idea of new beginnings today.

And I decided to act on it. I was detail cleaning all morning. I was wiping down the chest of drawers in my bedroom. I ran a wet sponge along the varnished wood. And just like that, I saw a silhouette of my reflection staring back at me. It grabbed my attention.

For reasons I can't explain, seeing the stillness of my reflection reminded me that change is a behaviour. As I stared at myself, I understood that deep personal growth comes from action. That's not to say there's something wrong with having a profound realisation. In fact, nothing can change without first shifting your perception. Being able to change your perception is the spark to creating something new.

But deep meaningful transformation comes from action. Amazing things can happen when a profound realisation is met with intent and purpose. Living out new beginnings is more than just words; it is a behaviour. And as funny as it sounds, I remembered all of that in the blink of a realisation. As quick as a thought is formed, I saw what I needed to do to create something new.

And then impulse kicked in. The thin layer of water that captured my reflection started to dissipate. Out of nowhere, I felt compelled to act. I immediately grabbed a handful of garbage bags from the kitchen. I rushed back to the drawers and impulsively started scooping all of my clothes into the bags. I found myself doing the same thing in the wardrobe.

Without thinking, I threw several bags of clothes into the car and drove straight to the nearest Salvation Army centre. It wasn't until I had handed them over the counter and walked back to the car that I realised what just happened. I'd effectively given away most of my clothes. I wasn't even sure I had any pyjamas left for tonight.

It was time for a quick shop. First thing I saw when I got to the shopping centre was a barber. Astrid used to cut my hair; I hadn't been to a proper barber or hairdresser in years. I walked straight in and sat down. When asked what sort of haircut I wanted, I just told the guy to choose.

He smiled and said thanks.

Later that day I ate food I'd never tried. I bought clothes I'd never normally wear. I even started conversations with random strangers, and sang out loud whenever I wanted. Before heading home, I felt incredibly blessed to be in the position to do all of those things. And I decided to act upon the feeling of gratitude. I came across a charity-stall in the shopping centre. Without hesitating, I signed over some money to them.

Today was absolutely amazing. And all of it unfolded from a willingness to act upon the idea of creating a new beginning.

As I sit here, ready to sign off for the night, I am reminded of how profound the nuances of life can be. New beginnings don't always require a cataclysmic shift of consciousness. Not always. Sometimes the smallest things make the biggest difference.

THE LIGHT *of* RELATIONSHIPS

Monday (*3:30am without sleep*)

And then there are moments in life when you just freak out.

I guess technically, this is the first time in 48 days that I failed to write to myself date-by-date. As I sit here, it's actually Tuesday morning before dawn. Not only did I fail to write before midnight, I almost deleted everything I have written up to this point.

I give myself permission to push on as normal because I haven't slept yet. So from a certain point of view, I am still writing about Monday before I sleep it off. It's a flimsy justification but it's the one I choose.

Surprisingly, today kicked my arse. I don't always reflect on the difficult times. But that doesn't mean they don't happen. This story, and my life as I write about it, has nothing to do searching for constant happiness. That idea is synthetic and lacks authenticity. I will not ignore the difficult times under a veil of plastic bliss. There's no evolution in that.

It's funny though. All of the great things that come from writing this dialogue seem flimsy whenever I'm deeply lost. When the noise of doubt is kicking my backside, I feel slightly embarrassed. I couldn't bring myself to open the laptop and start writing today. I felt angry and defeated at the idea of it.

And that shocked me too. I haven't felt angry or defeated for a while. The feelings blindsided me. Rather than trusting my impulse to delete everything, I stayed away from the house. I wanted to avoid doing something stupid.

This is what happened.

I got called to a meeting about a return to work plan. And I immediately freaked out. I'm a 38-year-old man with relatively strong shoulders. Often, I'm not without insight. Normally, I'm able to find solutions to difficult problems. And yet today, one simple phone call about work almost had me hiding under the bed.

A whirlwind of emotions took hold. Somehow I felt like a victim. Part of me expected this. I've been thinking about my job quite often lately. I've been worried it was time to face it and I didn't feel ready.

I always get completely exhausted when my feelings rule the day. Everything has an accent of strain to it when my emotions take over. It's weird that a job I once did with confidence could make me so anxious.

It's almost four o'clock in the morning as I write this. In roughly six hours I have to be at a meeting about my job. I'm freaking out because I have no idea how to answer the questions I'll be asked. I don't know what I'm meant to do.

This is the first time that writing in this forum has not brought clarity. It is the first time I resent being here. I'm logging off before I do something stupid.

THE LIGHT *of* RELATIONSHIPS

Tuesday

I haven't felt nerves like that for a long time.

I attended the meeting as requested. It was awful. I felt small and pent-up throughout the whole thing. As predicted, I was unable to answer any of the questions about returning to work. The meeting was not overly confrontational, but I was pushed slightly to consider my future employment. When I thought about the idea of returning, I felt cornered and anxious.

Reliving the struggle was terrible. I was forced to put my work hat back on, and I didn't like it one bit. I felt like an imposter in my own skin.

Towards the end of the meeting, I was asked to take some time to consider my options. Initially, I was just relieved to be getting out of there. But as I got up to go, I found the answer that had been eluding me all morning. I knew what I had to do. I heard two words: 'New Beginnings'

And then I felt a deep sense of relief. I calmly explained that I had no need to consider a return to work plan because I had no intention of ever returning. As soon as I said it out loud the possibility of returning had been extinguished. That chapter of my life was finished.

Without waiting for a response, I walked out of the office. I drove home in silence. I couldn't get the smile off my face. My awareness felt alert again. There was an all too familiar light of awareness everywhere. For some reason, I had a heightened sense of things again. I welcomed the ethereal shift in my reality. I had missed it.

I knew a significant chapter of my life had closed. I would never again identify with the job I had done for so long. I also realised the man I once was for Astrid has changed. In fact, the way I relate to Jess and Haylie (and the rest of my family) has dramatically shifted as well. Who I was, in the relative world, is no longer. And all I saw was a light of possibility. Where I'm headed is in motion now. It's beneath my feet. It's time now to embrace a new beginning.

As I accepted all of that, something weird happened. I was almost home, but something made me pull into our local café. I walked in without really knowing why. I stood quietly after ordering a coffee. But I felt conspicuous so

I went to leave. As I got to the exit, I saw a post on a noticeboard. 'Labrador puppies for sale.' The address was just around the corner. I went straight over.

It took about 10 seconds to choose the little man I would eventually take home. He was a little black labra-cutie with a tiny white sliver on his chest. If I'm honest, I think he picked me. The little guy plodded over to me straight away and started rag dolling my shoelaces. Evidently, the decision had been made.

As I went to leave, I remembered something important. I quickly called out to the owner of the littler: 'Wait hang on, when was the little guy born?' The reply I got was shockingly obvious: The 28th of July, just before five o'clock.

As I was getting into my car, I smiled and said under my breath: 'Of course he was.'

CHAPTER TEN

Ethereal Break

'When you trust someone with everything you have it is not difficult to find that within yourself'

THE LIGHT *of* RELATIONSHIPS

Wednesday

In many ways, I am grateful everything that's happened didn't come at a higher price. I woke this morning with a deep sense of purpose. I was fuelled by the vastness of the unknown. I took a deep breath out of relief. The ethereal break seemed like freedom at play.

However, I know that I only find myself here after hitting rock bottom. What my family and I went through was terrible. When I look back, all I see is darkness. But at the same time, I'm fortunate it wasn't worse. No one got seriously injured or permanently damaged. As it turns out, that wasn't required in order to wake from my slumber.

It was the little things that made the biggest difference. When I contemplate that, I feel protected and comforted. I feel guided by something that is devoid of confusion and doubt. It's difficult to pinpoint what I'm referring to. But either way, I feel very grateful.

I guess the growth I've experienced over the past two months comes from trusting something bigger than my doubts and worries. When I say that, I think about the ninth of August. The relief that came from detaching from my thoughts was a game-changer.

Every line in this story is but an 'echo of influence' from what took place when I detached from the potency of my thoughts. I saw a light of awareness that was connected to something much bigger than the smallness of doubt. I saw something exactly 42 days ago that was separate to what we think and feel.

'Doubt, Anger, Confusion, Worry'

These feelings have stopped me for long enough now.

Thursday

Man, did I spiral out of control last Monday.

It was a perfect illustration of how certain feelings can thwart someone's fulfilment. The whole 'return to work meeting' really caught me by surprise. Letting go of that part of my life feels amazing. I'm not entirely sure what the future holds on a vocational level. But I also don't care that much. The manner in which I fill my days (this dialogue) is sustaining me. More deeply than anything else I have taken on.

Yet, three days ago I seriously almost deleted every page of this thing. Coming from a place of doubt, I thought the lines of this story were an imposter in my life. I felt embarrassed about how I fill my days. And I almost surrendered to that reality. But something bigger than the noise of doubt stopped me from deleting the past seven weeks.

Monday night, just before midnight, I had resigned myself to the fact that I wasn't going to reflect in writing. Making the decision left me feeling disappointed. But I was too angry to care. I knew breaking the commitment would be a showstopper. But initially, I just felt indignant about it. I blamed an unnamed-source, or something like it, for how I felt.

I ignored the choice of my life. I did what I have done so often in the past. I went outside and started shouting at the stars. I questioned what I was meant to do. I blamed the circumstance I faced for the feelings I had. It was just about the smallest I've felt since the beginning of this process.

For a brief moment, I forgot that growth is entirely about choice.

As I sit here talking about it, I can see things more clearly. I understand now that being embarrassed is a question of perspective. How I view this story is a choice. I can look at it with soft eyes or judge it harshly. I forgot that how I view the possibility for this dialogue could be precisely the same as how I view the possibilities for my life. It's entirely about choice.

Three nights ago I forgot that. I got swept up with emotion. Standing outside in the middle of the night, I heard not one single piece of insight. I waited for comfort but none came. I smacked the post I was leaning on and decided to go back inside. I was going to erase everything I had written. I told myself it was time to grow up. I trusted the doubt and anger that fuelled my thoughts.

But as I turned my back on the stars, something happened. I went to open the front door but something stopped me. What happened is the reason I am sticking to the commitment I made here. I heard a voice. And it was much bigger than any noise of doubt. Four words that changed everything:

'I need you here'

And I intend to find out what that means.

Friday

I'm grateful my parents are two of my closest confidants. They have not lived together for more than three decades. But I have remained close to each of them. I worked with so many children who never knew the grace of having gentle parents. I'm grateful my folks have been significant mentors throughout my life.

My mother (Anne) is such a huge support. I can't say just how often she has shown up because her instincts told her to. As I've mentioned, she is a clairvoyant. Mum has spent the past 28 years in the service of others. She has devoted her life to bringing comfort and peace to as many people as are willing to listen.

This morning she sent me a message asking if I've been out in nature lately. She told me to meet her at the beach. When you trust someone with everything you have it's not difficult to find that within yourself. I knew, with the certainty of a sunrise, that what was to come would matter.

Growing up with someone who is deeply spiritual can be quite interesting. I have heard and seen some things that are beyond the normal limits of doing your chores and brushing your teeth before bed. I have been stumped by the unexplainable more times than I can remember. I guess at some point, I should stop being shocked by the surprises.

As soon as I saw Mum today, she asked if I've got to the 'gritty stuff' yet. Without any confidence, I chuckled as if I knew what she was talking about. But then I had to ask what she meant.

Mum told me to pay attention to a man across the street. He was talking on his mobile phone. He was actually being quite loud. This unnamed guy was pacing around, waving his arms aggressively at nothing. He didn't look well to be honest. He was slightly overweight with a red complexion and thinning, oily hair. It looked like he could use a few days in bed. After seeing him, I wondered why I hadn't noticed him sooner. He was quite animated. It was difficult to ignore.

Mum asked if I've been there before. Without hesitating, I said 'too often.' She replied: 'And you think that's you, you think that's all there is…'

Shocked by the surprises.

As if she had been reading this dialogue, Mum asked if I was prepared to wake up to the truth of my life. She questioned if I had the fortitude to see beyond the fiction I created. She pointed out that what happened in the second week of August was just the beginning. She explained that I was always on a collision course with the status quo.

That's when I felt my eyes starting to sting. Mum gently explained what happened with Astrid, and everything that followed was inevitable. She reminded me that all things in life happen for a reason. But that does not imply that any one of us is a victim to circumstance.

She nudged her head towards the guy across the street, and said that too often, we think we are what 'happens to us.' That, in this partnership of life, too many of us believe we are our circumstance. She said it was time for me to look beneath my feelings and find the truth.

That, like everything in nature, thoughts and feelings pass by with the changing winds. She challenged me to look beneath the cycle of my life.

She finished by saying: 'That's the gritty stuff.'

Ripples of Stillness

Saturday

Look beneath your feelings and see the truth.

The idea of that gave everything a silent edge today. It almost had me looking over my shoulder at different times. Like all things in nature, our thoughts and feelings pass by with the changing winds. Contemplating that, gave the day a silent disposition. I was compelled to be outdoors today. I went to Mundaring Weir. For some reason, I wanted red earth under my feet and the calmness of water in my eyes. I remembered Nicola's words:

'Remain heavy on the earth'

I didn't feel lofty or confused today. It was the silence that grabbed my attention. I felt grounded by everything around me. It seemed like the experience of meditation happened to me. Nature had me today. The stillness everywhere was like a blank canvas. The noises around me seemed like brush strokes in my imagination.

To begin with, all I could do was sit down and close my eyes. The moment demanded it of me. I felt something very deep. I found myself beyond the impulse to act on what was happening. I had no desire to react to anything. The moment quite simply needed to be noticed.

As weird as it sounds, it felt like my mother was with me, or at least her message was present. I felt a gentle awareness in the centre of my forehead. Almost like a pressing sensation. I became aware of the warmth in the centre of my chest. I heard my heartbeat without needing to check anything. I could hear the dirt crackle beneath my feet, the trees creak gently in the wind. Somehow the noise within was precisely the same as the sounds around me. I felt young inside.

It's difficult to find the words.

I guess it was a feeling that required no action. I had a deep sense of connection and peace that needed nothing from me. The moment was present, and it was daring me to join in. I could feel a type of stillness calling on me to be silent. It was a moment devoid of time. It was new and untouched.

The awareness I saw could never be tampered with. Yet it remains wise. It owns the stories of the world. It represents all things. It was new and untouched, yet it has always been there.

Just before my corporeal reality kicked back in, my family and friends drifted through my mind. I saw them smiling at me as if they were passing clouds. As the wind touched my arm, I felt their gentle influence. Astrid, Jess and Haylie splashed through my sight as I heard different animals and insects at play. Their presence seemed like colours to my eyes.

The events of the ninth of August crossed my mind. For a brief moment, I remembered what was forgotten. And then something familiar seemed to touch my shoulder. It broke my ethereal gaze. But before that happened, I saw a truth that was difficult to ignore.

We are not our thoughts and feelings. Beneath our emotional outbursts and troublesome thoughts, there is something much bigger at play. We are deeper than our doubts, stronger and more resolute than our worries. And there is an untouched part of life that is daring us to open our eyes.

Sunday

The spiritual residue from yesterday is still with me. I can't shake the feeling that someone familiar was there. On a rational level I realise that wasn't the case. But at the same time, there's an itch I can't scratch here.

I have been blanketed by a feeling of atonement all day. Nothing is going on tonight, but I still feel excited as I sit here writing these words. The stillness of the outside world keeps flashing through my mind. I keep getting little pockets-of-peace at random times. It's great to tap into what I felt yesterday.

A lot of what I am experiencing lately is difficult to explain. Sometimes mere words don't cut it. There are quite a few paradoxes. I can't afford to look at things rigidly any more. When trying to explain the unexplainable, I guess everything is on the table. My regular penchant to have things be 'one way or another' no longer exists. The ultimate reality of life is not black and white. I see now that in order to move forward, I need to remember that life is not about hard-and-fast rules.

We are not our feelings. At the very least, we are not our emotional outbursts. Constantly reacting to different feelings is a thin reality. Reacting with emotions as if they just happen to you lacks depth.

Beneath the expression of our feelings there is a part of life that is always still. Beyond our daily emotional reactions, there is a deep untouched part of life that is resting peacefully. This reality stretches out from the horizon. Its vibration reaches the infinite nature of the universe. It can never be tampered with.

And it is found within.

The Light *of* Relationships

Monday

I used to think it was a good thing to be an emotional person. At least it was better than being robotic about life. I don't have the words to describe just how often I got carried away with my emotions. I confused being passionate with reacting emotionally. In many ways, my life was fortified by a series of clichés. I told people that 'what you see is what you get.' I found comfort in proclaiming that 'I wear my heart on my sleeve.' Although quite often, I found myself in vigorous debates, I always felt justified because 'I won't pretend to be someone I'm not.' My life was more about hiding behind the statements of others rather than being authentic.

Last Monday was a perfect example of when my emotions got the better of me. I felt anger, disappointment, frustration and doubt. I trusted those feelings. Perhaps it's more precise to say I trusted there was nothing else. I blamed the day. I didn't see the choice beyond what I felt. I surrendered to the worry as if something happened to me.

Getting swept away with emotion takes the responsibility of your life out of your hands. It's a mask, a way of hiding. Truth is, there's no unnamed source that can create doubt from within. There's no cliché that can justify living small. It's all about choice.

I think back to the countless times that I got carried away with my emotions. The examples are like stars in the sky. There are too many to comprehend. I have felt frustrated professionally. Too often I've felt impatient and angry in traffic. I have known disappointment from friendships. I have tasted heartbreak and sadness from relationships.

I look back at last Monday again. It's the most recent example I can think of when my negative feelings took hold. I was so frustrated and angry. What I felt sabotaged everything.

I could have justifiably said that 'I am angry.' I assumed 'I was disappointed.' I felt cornered and pent up. It was horrible. I can feel my forehead tighten as I think about it. But its incomplete to assume those negative feelings were all there was. Subconsciously blaming outside influences for what I went through is a mask. It's a way of hiding behind something small.

What can't be ignored is that those feelings came from within. In truth, I am not the feeling of anger. I am bigger than the feeling of disappointment. Heartbreak does not define me. Feelings are simply indications of something. They are a creative force of communication. They can be a trigger-point for action. But they do not define us.

If I feel anger, it is incomplete to say 'I am angry.' I am not anger any more than I'm an itch on my leg. Assuming that 'I am what I feel' is a pathway to living small. The mere suggestion of it is about suppression. The statement 'I am disappointed' helps keep that reality alive. The words create it, they sponsor the feeling.

It's more precise to say that you 'have' feelings. It's cleaner to acknowledge that you notice certain feelings or emotions. To step aside from your feelings and observe them creates a blank canvas for your life. And the colours of creation can be whatever you choose.

Tuesday

Beyond the preoccupations of doubt, there is something much bigger at play. Your feelings can be a trigger-point to living consciously. Again, I recognise that so-called negative feelings have nothing to do with being bad. There is nothing wrong with feeling anything. Stepping aside from your feelings is about seeing they are a natural part of life.

It's quite proportional to have feelings of anger and disappointment sometimes. Stepping aside from your feelings is not about wishing for constant bliss. It's more about taking responsibility for how your life plays out.

Adding guilt and resistance to feelings that do not serve you is futile. It just creates a self-perpetuating cycle of negativity. Feelings such as anger, worry and doubt are sticky enough. They do not need any help from us. Reacting emotionally during difficult times makes things more difficult. The stories we attach to the difficult times determine how they are played out. All feelings are a natural part of the human experience. We can afford to simply leave them alone.

I remember part of a quote…

> *'When one has feelings and appreciates them, one is free…'*
> Buddha

I dare to imagine what life would be like if we all just appreciated our feelings. If, rather than adding resistance, we met our thoughts and feelings with unreserved gratitude. Try to imagine what would happen if we brought a light of appreciation to the natural expression of our lives. Even just writing about it has me leaning against Nirvana. The mere mention of such a thing straightens my soul.

And all of that is meaningless unless it is shared with others.

CHAPTER ELEVEN

Authenticity of Love

'Thoughts and feelings are not to be dismissed. They are the only way in which we perceive life.'

Wednesday

Rhetorically speaking, how on God's green earth am I meant to appreciate the feelings of others if I don't appreciate my own feelings?

I can't reach prosperity and fulfilment in a relationship if I don't identify those virtues within. I started out this month on a quest to understand intimate relationships better. As always, I didn't really know what to expect. I just went with the flow.

I've spent the better part of the month unpacking what makes me tick. It was not the original plan. Initially, I assumed that looking into what makes a relationship work would involve unpacking the behaviour of others. I thought it would be about what makes someone else happy.

In fact, I have spent my entire life thinking that way. I thought a successful relationship was about putting others first. I assumed intimacy was about submitting to the needs and wants of 'that special someone.' I was convinced meaningful connections were built around trying to figure out how to please someone without them having to ask. The focus was always outsourced. And the chorus was always the same...

'If you loved me'

However, my well-intentioned theories always collapsed in a dust pile of disappointment. History indicates that outsourcing love was not sustainable. That's not to say that selfishness thwarted my relationships. All of my past relationships ended up being rather underwhelming. But it wasn't for selfish reasons. It was more about the authenticity of love being misrepresented. The spark in my relationships seemed to diminish through a lack of authenticity.

The idea of submitting to something, so that love was proved, was never sustainable. It felt disingenuous to test the boundaries of love.

But that wasn't the major problem I faced.

Issues always started to arise because I couldn't sell the message. And that's because I wasn't clear about what it should be. Deep down I knew that authentic love did not require validation. But at the same time, I used all of my past relationships to try to prove that theory. And in doing so, without intention, I started testing the boundaries of love.

Simply writing all of that does my head in. I had to re-read what I just wrote several times in order to understand it.

And come to think of it… That is exactly how I treated my relationships. I felt confused about how to operate within them, and I kept re-reading the situation over and over again to understand it. The whole process was about testing something. It was entirely about validating something to myself.

I thought if I was not with someone special there must be something wrong with me. Getting into a relationship was about feeling complete. And as soon as one had settled down enough, I set about testing the limits of that theory. Everything was predicated on outsourcing how I felt. I used relationships to reinforce my feelings. I used others to feel worthy.

But after everything that's happened recently, I'm starting to see something deeper. Love requires none of that. It cannot be tested because it has no limits. Testing love is an illusion. It can't be done. Truth is, I wasn't simply trying to challenge love within a relationship. I was testing myself. I was questioning my own self-worth through the process of intimacy.

And the eyes of love remained steadfast regardless.

THE LIGHT *of* RELATIONSHIPS

Thursday

I woke before the sun today.

I was preoccupied about something. Without knowing why, I kept thinking back to the last time I saw Tristan. It was about four weeks ago. We've talked on the phone and emailed often since then. But for some reason I couldn't stop thinking about the last time I saw him. I remember Tristan asking me to go easy on myself. He said something about deserving Astrid. He talked about honouring love.

> *'The answer isn't found in how amazing Astrid is. It's not about giving her something in order to win her back. And until you know what all of that means, don't do anything stupid.'*
> Tristan

It's been exactly 33 days since those words resonated through my mind. His message is about self-worth I think. That idea kept me busy today. I needed to talk to Bryce or Tristan for some reason. After taking Jess and Haylie to school, I went to contact them. I opened my email with the intention of seeing if either of them was available for a chat. That was when my day pivoted towards the incredible.

Before I go on, I'll point out that Tristan and Bryce are two of my closest friends, but they have very little to do with each other. They lead very separate lives. Coupled with that, neither of them have anything to do with my extended family. That's just the way it's always been.

Now, we push on with what happened this morning.

I was just about to send the guys a message. As soon as I opened my email, I noticed that each of them had contacted me already. I instantly felt my eyes sharpen. I fumbled through reading their messages. I couldn't believe what they had to say. In their own words, Tristan and Bryce challenged me to look into my own self-worth.

I was stunned. I just sat there shaking my head in disbelief. I actually questioned what was real for a second. I couldn't stop reading their emails. I was trying to make sense of everything. And then I got another message.

This is what it read:

'I trust you found some answers last weekend. I was pleased to feel your joy. But I need something from you now. It's time for you to follow this to the end.

Imagine all you know to be true about God. Reflect for a moment on how God must feel about life. About the people you love - Astrid, Jess, Haylie and everyone else.

Consider that you've always known everything is connected in a harmonious play of life.

Remember that, life itself is by God's design.

And then imagine for a second, that for some reason, God decided not to include you in His plans. Knowing everything you know, explain why God would do that.

It's time for you to conceptualise your worthiness.'

Love Mum

And I freaked out!

I couldn't handle it. I went to shoot up from my chair, but all I could do was grab my fringe. I went to pick up the phone to ring everything, but I was unable to move because of nervous excitement. I simply couldn't believe what had just happened. It was too big. The whole thing was too much to comprehend. It felt like I was going to pop. I ran outside and screamed embarrassingly loudly. And in a blink, I found peace. I heard a clear message from within...

'You are precisely where you should be. Doing exactly what you're meant to.'

And in that moment, nothing else mattered.

THE LIGHT *of* RELATIONSHIPS

Friday

For a brief moment yesterday I was left with nothing to worry about. I was complete without needing anything. In that very moment, I glimpsed the idea of realised potential. And before I talk about what it looked like, I need to say few things. To do so, I will back track slightly. I want to have a run at this thing.

Firstly, I reiterate that thoughts and feelings are not to be dismissed. In fact, it would seem they are the only way in which we perceive life. Our thoughts and feelings are a form of communication. Ultimately, they are how we express life. What we think is a creative force. Our thoughts determine what we say and how we say it. Our feelings can be used exactly the same way. They can reveal the truth just as much as they can shield us from it.

These things are unstoppable. It's simply a question of how they are accomplished. We can play out our thoughts and feelings with intention. Or we can live an illusion that we are simply victims to circumstance. We can live consciously or not.

Secondly, I remind myself that a relationship, if chosen with intent, can be one of the most authentic ways to express who we are. To explain, I will unpack the opposite. This is what I brought to my relationships…

I expect the woman I love (Astrid) to fill a void that I created. And when she fails to do so, I blame the inadequacies of the relationship for the source of my discontent. I start the relationship with a lack of self-worth, and blame the person I'm with for not being worthy of filling the void. The whole thing is predicated on not being whole to begin with. It's all one big test, and it has nothing to do with the ultimate truth of who we are.

Thirdly, the search for being whole cannot be outsourced. The idea of being complete has nothing to do with searching for something. To search for fulfilment is to concede it is not there to begin with. It is a universal declaration that you are not fulfilled.

Waking up to your own worthiness is about never again searching for completion. But instead, embracing that your very presence is what gives life value. The deepest value of all things is that life exists. To meet that reality with appreciation is a manifestation of freedom.

And I am only able to say all of that through the expression of my thoughts and feelings. I'm only able to recognise the miracle of life by creating it from within. These things are not about self-gratification though. Embracing your inner self-worth has nothing to do with how great you are. It's not about being 'the one' or standing out from the pack.

It's entirely about understanding your highest reality. It comes from recognising the source of all things. Thoughts and feelings come and go like the changing-winds of nature. Beneath that reality, the truth dares to be recognised. The idea of being complete is found within. Realised potential is a cultivation of the highest order.

And the highest reality of life is love.

THE LIGHT of RELATIONSHIPS

Saturday

Pope John Paul II said something similar to this…

> *'Life comes from God: It is His image and imprint, as a sharing in this breath of life. God therefore is the soul of this life…'*

To understand the ultimate purpose behind all human relationships is to understand your self worth. And the expression of those things comes from within. The purpose behind a relationship cannot be tested. Nor can a relationship be used for anything. Not in a way that counts.

Intimacy requires no validation. It exists only to be experienced. It is neither fortified nor weakened by the opinions of the world. And the virtues of intimacy exist as a gift to every living soul.

Such is the ultimate purpose behind all human relationships. At the deepest level, an intimate relationship exists so that we might remember who we are. It's less about 'giving and receiving' and more about something infinitely larger. The idea of 'giving and receiving' is about getting something from a relationship. In truth, getting something from an outside source can't be done. It's an illusion. And the idea of it removes us from what's really going on.

The truth of our lives is that we are here to experience love. Not in order to get something, but because that is who we are. The deepest form of self-worth is the expression of love. Relationships exist so that we may remember that. They are about a connection with love. They are about the expression and exploration of our true nature.

In truth, life comes from love. It is Her image and imprint, as a sharing in this breath of life. Love therefore is the soul of this life.

That is who we are.

Sunday

You better believe I was up before the sun today.

I mean my God! What an amazing, unbelievably incredible experience this process has been. It feels like it's happened to me. Despite everything the past month has revealed, I still feel like this experience is not of my doing. And for now, I'm not going to tamper with that. Sometimes it feels like I'm just taking the minutes here. But I'm not interested in unpacking that just yet. Things are happening way too fast to slow down for those questions right now.

Looking into what makes a relationship work was exhilarating to say the least. I remember what I wrote earlier. 'I can go from relationship breakups, to relationship breakthroughs.' I have woken to some pretty significant stuff. I have changed my outlook dramatically on quite a few things.

If I'm honest, I miss Astrid a lot after the week I just had. I miss our relationship. We've been sending each other messages and emails lately. It feels good to have a line of contact with her. She told me yesterday that she is working away again. Apparently, she is away for the next fortnight. That just comes with her job at this time of year.

Part of me thinks it's a good thing. I have absolutely no intention of mugging her with all of this stuff. It's too much – it's too huge. Instinctively, I know Astrid needs subtlety and gentle things at the moment. She is walking her own path, in order to find her own way. And I will not sabotage that.

However, I do miss her terribly. On some level, I wish I could share everything with her. But for now I will leave that alone as well.

So much has happened in such a short time...

The innocence of the morning sun is a beautiful thing. It has a silence that's nothing short of Godly. After waking, I sat outside thinking about everything that's happened. From the backdrop of dawn, the events of the past two months drifted through my mind. It was like watching a slideshow.

THE LIGHT *of* RELATIONSHIPS

It feels like a lifetime has passed since I saw the reflection of heartbreak in my eyes. I remember that morning vividly. My lifeless eyes reflected the sorrow I felt. As I gazed at the horizon remembering, I saw Astrid's face looking at me. I love her so much. Her spirit is completely beautiful. It's difficult to describe how much she means to me.

Once again, I will simply let my fingers explain.

Imagine the light of all relationships found a voice.

Allow your imagination to see the 'light of relationships' stretch out from behind the horizon. Picture the light becoming one with all that is. The 'light of relationships' becomes self-aware for the purpose of a conversation. Instantly and without fear, the light sought an audience with the 'eyes of sorrow.' The same eyes that reflected my world not so long ago.

'Why will you not look at me?' The light asked gently. *'Because I have failed you.'* replied the eyes of sorrow.

'That is a big accomplishment. I am the deepest form of God's communication; how have you failed me?' asked the light.

'I left you, and in doing so your light has escaped my eyes. I reflect a lifeless reality now. That is why I cannot bring myself to look at you. That is how I have failed you.'

'My beautiful friend, you cannot fail me. I am here to show you who you really are. I have come to offer you the opposite of what you see. I am your true nature. If you would but look up from what you see, I will make you shine again.'

'I dare not, for I am not worthy.' the eyes explained.

At that precise moment, the *light of all relationships* blanketed the world, making it impossible for the eyes of sorrow to live small. *'You are worthy of all that I am. You exist for no other reason but to see that we are one. Look into my eyes so that you may find yourself again.'*

The eyes of sorrow, amazed to hear that the deepest form of God's communication had eyes as well, blinked with excitement. And the gaze of sorrow was lifted.

Instinctively, the eyes moved into the horizon of light. They were immediately filled with wonderment. The lifeless small reality that once was had disappeared. The eyes became one with everything they saw. They were a perfect reflection of God's deepest form of communication. And just like that, they were filled with love.

Shining brightly now, the gaze of the eyes stretched out with anticipation. Almost immediately, something grabbed its attention. A scent began to stir. From behind the horizon, the eyes looked upon the voice that came. It was the comfort of love expressed.

It was the beauty of Astrid's soul.

PART THREE

October

The Energy of Love

CHAPTER TWELVE

APPRECIATION OF LIFE

*'It is quite a thing to catch the awareness of gratitude.
There's nothing but light there.'*

Monday 1 October

It's almost as if I am creating my reality one word at a time.

I'm starting to see the creative force of what I say is actually life at play. It is within the lines of this story that I am finding out who I am. The accent and influence of your life can be played out in the conversations you have. And that reality is not exclusive to the outside world. It also applies to listening to your instincts.

I'm starting to see things very clearly. I'm waking up to everything around me. This dialogue as I write it is part of the growth of my soul. Although I did not set out to do that, it feels incredible. As I refer to things in this forum, they seem to be happening in everyday life. I'm noticing what I bring up, on any given day, actually becomes part of my experience.

As I reflect in writing, I reflect what I'm writing.

The whole thing is a cyclical process of creation. And it's one of the most amazing things I have experienced. It's like my fingertips are revealing my life to me. When I make what I'm doing here about the act of creation, I automatically blow the lid off all forms of limitation.

Since I started this conversation two months ago, I have reflected on the importance of cleaning all aspects of my life. I have continually referred to the virtues of starting things anew. When I communicate from a blank page, I am able to experience whatever I choose.

Each page here starts the same way the freshness of the morning does. My fingers become a paintbrush to my insights. The lines of this story are the colours of my experience. My insights are forming a foundation. I am giving them room to explore what they see.

When I make this dialogue about the act of creation, I am restricted only by my ability to communicate. The story of my life is just the beginning. When I start from nothing, the universe becomes my playground. Two months ago, I started out assuming I would reflect on my experience. I have come to understand the complete opposite is more precise.

'I experience what I reflect'

And it's time to hunker down.

Tuesday

No more equivocations. No more second-guessing.

I got a lot from being honest. The stuff I was doing to keep my life small becomes less potent after I square-off with it. I call it forward for the purpose of a conversation. Not to belittle myself, but for the purposes of growth. It's a process of evolution through being honest.

Growth is about dropping the things I've been clinging to. Letting go of the idea that I have all the answers to begin with reveals everything else to me. I get to explore the possibilities of life once I stop ambushing it with my internal resume. And gratitude sits beneath those things.

My penchant of clinging to my insecurities seems small in the face of gratitude. Living with appreciation reminds me of something familiar. I become part of a partnership with life, rather than a subject of proving something to the world. Gratitude is the light in faith. To truly appreciate your life is to surrender your insecurities. To supplicate with gratitude is how miracles happen.

When your insights start with an accent of appreciation they are impossible to ignore. The voice of my instincts has never been louder than they are now. I am playing witness to the conviction of them. When I listen to my instincts with certainty, all I see is light. There is nothing but light in the certainty of gratitude. And it stretches out forever.

It's appropriate that I started this dialogue in the eighth month of the year. The number eight represents the symbol for infinity. The infinite nature of life is one big play of gratitude. And it's time to explore that.

I'm bringing God into the conversation now.

Wednesday

I'm not here to talk about a God of limitations.

Acknowledging your beliefs starts with recognising you have them. There is a major difference between looking into your beliefs and doubting them. When I start thinking about the infinite nature of the universe, I don't know where to begin. It gives me a moment's pause to contemplate the infinite possibilities of God.

Not knowing where to begin led me to a memory that almost seems a bit conveniently clichéd. Although I like to think of myself as a 'rough and tumble' Aussie bloke, today I couldn't stop thinking about an Oprah show from a while ago. The episode was about near-death experiences.

To begin with, everything about the episode seemed normal enough. Most of the guests talked about having a new outlook. Everyone seemed to have a deeper sense of faith after his or her experience. But then things got really interesting. The last guest was a man named John Diaz. I think he was a businessman. He might have been close to retirement age. I remember thinking he was softly spoken, but he still had confidence.

His story was slightly different. John was in a plane crash. Lots of people died, but he managed to get out through the emergency exit. He remembered looking down the belly of the plane before escaping the wreckage. He could see people burning alive. He recalled looking through all of the flames and smoke as he watched people die.

John spoke softly about seeing bright orbs leaving their bodies. He said some of the auras were bigger and brighter than others. His story was slightly different because he wasn't prepared to admit, beyond a reasonable doubt, that what he saw was a miracle. When asked what he took from his experience, John said he thought the brightness of people's auras must have been a reflection of how they had lived. He humbly said he was going do his best to live a life where his aura was very bright at the time of his passing.

When it comes to life's deeper purpose, I can't help but think about that story. John's experience wasn't about limitation or validation. It was about accepting that there is a light within each of us. It's about daring to believe that the essence of who you are shines in accordance with how you live.

Imagine what would happen if we all conducted ourselves, knowing for certain, that our soul wants to shine as brightly as a star.

Just imagine this:

'How you behave determines how brightly you shine'

When it comes to contemplating God, I dare to believe life could be that simple. It's true that sometimes I don't know where to begin when it comes to unpacking things to do with God and life's deeper purpose. But I know, without question, there is a light of wonderment to those things.

And from the stillness of certainty, I reach out to embrace the light of responsibility for my life. Not only for the cultivation of my soul but because it might just be possible that ultimately, how we behave in this life will expand the light of God.

Thursday

I have never questioned God's existence.

Nor do I dismiss the expression of faith by another. It's not for me to invalidate another person's faith. Dismissing someone else's beliefs so I feel better about my own is not faith at all. It's a forgery of something smaller. And it's got more to do with my internal resume than anything else. The deepest form of faith has nothing to do with validation.

But I didn't always hold those views. Not so long ago, I was more critical of things I didn't understand. I was quick to strike down beliefs that were different to mine. I looked to passively separate myself from those who were stubborn with their opposition. I told myself they were missing the point.

I guess I started thinking about all of that quite a bit today. It's humbling to see how limited my views used to be. I spent the morning remembering how small I was keeping my life. And I decided to act.

I grabbed my car keys and went for a drive in the Swan Valley and the hills of Darlington. There is a type of tranquillity in nature that is nothing short of amazing. To meet nature with gratitude should be the eleventh commandment. Halfway through the drive I came to an intersection that had a small church on it. It was a beautiful rustic little building. Right in front of the intersection was a big sign: *'Atheists of the world relax, God believes in you.'*

I chuckled to myself without really knowing why. I think it had something to do with the idea of life having faith in life. It took me back to the 'first time of things' for some reason. And then I started thinking about the things that connect us.

Coming from a place of faith without reason can be difficult to unpack sometimes. It's a concept that's not easy to scoop up quickly. Often it requires broad thinking and a willingness to be soft. But I don't say that in order to dismiss the beliefs of others. Holding those values is not about making others less in order to feel better about anything.

Atheists of the world relax, God believes in you.

In many respects, it's wrong to say that an atheist doesn't believe in anything just because they don't believe in God. An atheist, by definition, doesn't believe in life after death. They choose not to believe in anything divine or God-like. They believe there is nothing beyond the life they live.

But none of that means an atheist is without faith. Most of the time, it can mean the complete opposite. Quite often, being an atheist is entirely about seeing the value in life. It can be about taking very little for granted for no other reason except that life exists. And coming from that place, it is about loving more and living with purpose.

I guess ultimately we're all not so different from each other. How a person's life plays out is a question of perspective and choice. No one sees life precisely the same way as someone else. Our uniqueness is a gift of the highest order. But none of that exists to divide us. Ultimately, we are all an expression of life. We are all playing out the fulfilment of what we believe.

Perhaps, no matter what we call it, that's God at play.

Friday

I decided to take this story on the road today.

I thought it would be rather old-school to visit our local library. There is a type of comfort found in a library that can't be found elsewhere. I think it's got something to do with being amongst the silent stories of the world.

In many ways, I have nothing but reverence for the voices of the past. A library is full of people willing to share themselves. It is a place where generosity and passion is stacked high. I'm only two months into this thing, and there is no audience here, but I can testify that writing takes advance participation. You have to be willing to let your instincts chase you down. It's a commitment that sometimes feels like a mountain.

And it blows my mind to think about the countless number of authors who didn't have the luxury of the internet when they wrote their stories. The internet gives all of us a library at our fingertips.

From a certain perspective, this dialogue is nothing more than an exercise in exploring my instincts. I am simply giving a voice to the things that I've always wondered about. Some days, I am reading non-stop before I reflect here. My nine-to-five responsibility is about exploring the things that fascinate me. And I have the world's biggest library right here.

Google rocks!

But today I decided to walk the aisles of my fascinations. So much can be gained from engaging in your life. Being willing to give the deepest parts of you a voice is hugely rewarding. The most profound aspects to life are found within. You just have to pay attention.

While I was busy doing my thing at the library, I noticed an older lady doing the same. She was possibly in her 60s. She was sitting at the desk right in front of me. Throughout the day, I was taking breaks by stretching my posture and wandering around. However, this lady did not move from her seat. Hours went by, and she just sat quietly writing away with pen and paper.

Eventually my curiosity got the better of me. I kept looking over at this silent little busy-bee. I became distracted by my untouched thoughts. I couldn't stop staring at this mystery library companion. I started to feel a little rude. After a while, I shot up from my seat and went for another walk. It was clear I was distracting myself. I bought a bottle of water before returning to my desk. This had become thirsty work.

And then it hit me. I walked straight over to the lady and asked if she could use a drink. I handed her the bottle of water. Her eyes smiled as she whispered 'thank you.' After that, it didn't take long to refocus. Unsurprisingly, I got caught-up in what I was doing again. The outside world was not in my thoughts.

However, after a while something grabbed my attention. I looked up to see the lady standing at my desk with a piece of paper in her outstretched hand. I took it from her before she walked out of the library without saying a word.
I opened the folded piece of paper straight away.

It read: 'Do unto others. Thank you Brother.'

Saturday

> *Do unto others as you would have them do unto you...'*
> Matthew 7:12

I believe the intention of religion is to give people a sense of belonging. For me, religion is about a communion with God. And there are many ways in which that can be accomplished. Ultimately, the purpose behind all faith can be summed up by the golden rule.

When in doubt, treat people the way you want to be treated. It's a simple message that's echoed an eternity through almost every religion in the world. The golden rule could appropriately be viewed as the blueprint to all meaningful connections.

After yesterday's little gift, I started thinking about the expression of faith, and the idea of reaching fulfilment through it. And I'm not only referring to Christianity. I started thinking about the expression of faith everywhere. I've listened to the teachings of the Koran on an audio book. The idea of returning evil with good was mentioned several times. The golden rule:

> *'Love your brother as you love yourself'*
> Hadith 13

I guess if someone were to wake up to a spiritual truth, the spark would have to be about unity. I go to the teachings of Buddha. After his moment of enlightenment, Buddha spent 45 years reaching out to people. He went everywhere in India spreading messages of compassion, tolerance and love. When talking about cause and effect he said:

> *'Hurt not others in ways that you yourself would find hurtful.'*
> Buddha

Taoism was founded around the same time as Buddhism. It was over 500 years before Christianity would arrive. As I've said, the Tao Ti Ching is the second-most published book after the Bible. The golden rule of The Way is:

> *'Love the world as your own self; then you can truly care for all things'*
> Lao Tzu

Now, let's go to the most published book of all time. The Bible starts with the Torah. The Old Testament and Judaism have some beautiful messages, centred on the idea that people should treat each other the way they want to be treated.

> *'Love your neighbour as yourself...'*
> Leviticus 19:18

Hinduism could be the oldest religion. Some claim its ethereal law goes beyond human origins. There are some breathtaking messages to be found there.

> *'Where can we go to find God if we cannot see Him in our own hearts and in every living being.'*
> Swami Vivekananda

The branches of religion all seem to grow from the same tree of knowledge. And it's grounded in something separate to the nature of competitive division. The golden rule in almost all faith-based ideas is about connection and relationships. Spiritual faith is entirely about those things.

Despite the way in which we celebrate and honour our beliefs, we all seem to be honouring the same thing. It is the life force of connection that drives the human spirit. It is the essence of love that brings us together.

Perhaps we find ourselves here because eternity wanted a voice.

Sunday

I woke today feeling a bit emotionally thin.

Despite everything I've been engaging in recently, I started to feel a bit too cerebral for my own good. It's been a week without Jess and Haylie. Astrid is working away for another few days. I realised this morning that I haven't had much face-to-face contact with anyone for a while. Not in any kind of meaningful way.

My instincts have never been stronger. I've never been more certain and confident. Without needing to ask the world, I know the certainty I feel comes from engaging in life. My instincts are synchronised with how I picture my highest form of fulfilment. I am representing what matters the most to me with action. And the silence of my doubts and worries is the reward.

Coming from a place of certainty, I decided to clear something up today. Catching up with Bryce has occupied my thoughts recently. So today, we caught up.

As soon as Bryce saw me, he chuckled and said: 'You finally figured it out didn't you?' For some reason, I questioned him without needing to. Bryce said it was obvious I'd figured out how to leave myself alone. He smiled and shook my shoulders with excitement. I explained that I'm paying attention to what matters, that I'm living-out the idea of my highest reality. Bryce asked what that looked like in practical terms.

That's when I told him about this dialogue and everything that's been going on. I talked about detaching from my negative thoughts. I reflected about Thursday the ninth of August. I mentioned seeing nature at play at Mundaring Weir. I told him about recognising the true nature of my feelings. I explained what the light of relationships meant. And what the expression of it looked liked from my perspective. And finally, I said that I had let go of the relationship I once had with Astrid.

I haven't had a lot of practice talking about all that stuff. Consequently, the conversation was quite fast-paced. Bryce managed to keep up well enough. He has a world view beyond his years. I've always thought he was an old soul.

He has a considered disposition like no other.

After I unpacked the last two months, I asked if he understood. I acknowledged that everything I shared was a lot to take in. I finished by asking Bryce what reaching fulfilment looked like to him. And his answer made something surge.

He looked forward after taking a deep breath. I could tell he was about to speak from the relief that is found there. He said gently: 'Let life be this simple, to love another person is to see the face of God.'

I felt my posture surrender as something surged. It was gratitude. For the first time since I started this dialogue, I had surrendered to the process before me. Coming from the honesty of Bryce's answer, I felt a connection to something indiscriminately bigger than myself. I felt a pulse of gratitude surge through my bones.

Monday

Everything got ramped-up significantly two weeks ago after I nudged the idea of appreciating my own feelings. It was the idea of bringing a light of appreciation to the natural expression of our lives.

But that's not about chasing gratitude. And it's not about pushing anything away so you can feel happy all of the time either. It is about acceptance. It's about recognising the value in life, through the expression of it. It's about understanding the verbs of you.

The natural expression of our lives is played out through what we think and how we feel. Even if we don't act upon those things, we are still expressing ourselves. Even if we suppress our thoughts and feelings, we are still playing out our lives. Ultimately, we are constantly expressing ourselves no matter what. Inaction is a form of expression. It may not lead to anything new, but it is still a creation from within.

A grateful life is a free one.

To meet the blank canvas of your life with appreciation is a manifestation of freedom. It's not entirely for the sake of happiness though. It's more about owning how your life unfolds. And there is nothing but gratitude found behind that reality.

It is quite a thing to catch the awareness of gratitude. There's nothing but light there. But it has nothing to do with chasing anything down. And that's because the light in gratitude is not separate from you. It cannot be apprehended by anything. It can only be embraced through a complete acceptance of self.

Such are the verbs of God.

CHAPTER THIRTEEN

The Thread of Life

'The generosity of others can be where we find ourselves'

THE ENERGY *of* LOVE

Tuesday

When I think about faith, I defer to the need for fulfilment. The desire for fulfilment seems to be inherent in all of us. It is hard-wired into the psyche of everyone.

However, that does not rule out problematically destructive behaviours. In fact, the desire for fulfilment is sometimes the reason for those things. For 12 years, I worked with heaps of different families. I have seen some pretty full-on things from kids who only knew violence and deprivation. When a child grows up experiencing that stuff as the norm, they will naturally outsource it as they go through life. It takes a lot to get them to see past what they have learnt.

Often we will cling to what we know in order to remain comfortable, even if what we are clinging to is not therapeutic. The expression of drama and anger can be fulfilling to some people. I've seen it. Some people, and not just at-risk children, revel in the dramas they create. Sometimes it's the only comfort they have. The need for comfort and fulfilment seems to be the expression of our lives.

And I have not seen one single example where that does not apply. I'm not just referring to problematic behaviours. I'm talking about everything. I'm referring to all of us. And I base that on almost everyone I've met in my life.

So much of my adolescence was spent talking with strangers. Day-after-day I would sit with different people from all walks of life. I had countless conversations with people who were booked in to see my mother. Their waiting room was also our living room. Every day was full of brand new conversations. And I can say without flinching, that most of what I heard was the same.

People came because they were chasing comfort. They all needed to hear that they were on the right track with life. Almost everyone I met had booked in to have a reading for the same reason. They were looking to validate their lives. They all sensed there was something bigger, and they wanted to know if what they felt was justified. Said simply, they were chasing fulfilment.

And I have never heard a different story. I was never surprised by anything new. Yet because that was the case, I felt closer to everyone who shared with me. They echoed the picture I saw of the world. Their questions were also in the heart of me. Through hearing the stories of others, I became clearer about my own. And the thing that stood out the most was the importance of meaningful connections.

Working with at-risk children has shown me that sometimes a person's history can mean they face pathological issues. Those issues are not to be dismissed or minimised. But facing medical issues does not rule out the need for fulfilment. The want for fulfilment is a thread that connects all of us.

And I go now to find that in others.

Wednesday

The generosity of others can be where we find ourselves.

It's time to engage with the people in my life. Seeing Bryce the other day reinforced something important. Through sharing with him, I felt clearer about everything. It reminded me of the importance of reaching out to people. And I intend to take that to the next level. Moving forward, I will surrender my attention to the people in my life who make it so amazing.

First and foremost - my sister. As soon as we saw each other, Nicola acknowledged that I looked a little different. She suggested I find a way to live out what I'm doing for as long as possible. And then she threw a spontaneous little quiz my way. She asked me to explain why it was so important.

I said that I finally loved life, and my place in it; that I owed it to myself to live out my greatest potential. That's precisely when Nic ordered the champagne. And let me just say before I move on...

There is something beyond the importance of hashtags and retweets that waits for every single person. And it's not even that hard to find. Beyond our need for distraction, the opportunity for something meaningful awaits.

I asked Nic what her idea of fulfilment was.

And she stepped up to the podium in more ways than one. She was so generous with her answer. She said, that on a vocational level, she was never more fulfilled than when she was creating from nothing. She spoke about the gift of creation that sat within each of us. She linked it to the Creative Force of the Universe. I asked if she was happy to call that God. She said that our Catholic upbringing sometimes made her a bit restless about embracing that idea. But most of the time, she did not surrender to the doubt of that.

Nic echoed some of the words found here. She said that it was natural, and somewhat proportional, for a person to question exactly what God was. That in truth, often pretending you already have all of the answers was the very thing that kept you blind. She was comfortable looking into the nature of God, but that did not mean she doubted the love found there.

Without any arrogance, Nic said all that she was, came from all that was created. And on her best day, the deepest form of her fulfilment came from understanding that unchangeable fact. It was the stillness behind her words that grabbed me. I asked how she reconciled her upbringing with what she now believed. Nic waved her hand at my question as if it was an annoying fly. She answered firmly:

'The love of God knows nothing of guilt'

That's when I ordered more champagne.

THE ENERGY *of* LOVE

Thursday

I am here to say if you don't want to live small, engage in meaningful conversations. Go after sincerity with relentless intent. There's nothing but potency in doing that. If you recognise the amazing qualities in others, your life will become amazing. The archway to all of it is passion. Activate passion in your life, and you will find meaning.

I caught up with Tristan today.

I don't remember the last time we had a small conversation. We simply don't gossip or do weather reports. I am reminded that the accent and influence of your life is played out through the conversations you engage in. Whenever I talk with Tristan, I feel bigger and better about myself. He has a gift of sharing that is difficult to put into words.

For the most part, I asked the questions today. I started by asking the obvious one - what was his idea of realised potential. And when you call on Tristan with such things, he grows from the inside out.

He said his strength was found in the love of God. He said that without reservation. His conviction silenced me. I was left speechless. Only for a second or two. But then I heard Bryce's question run through my mind. I asked Tristan to explain what he meant on a practical level. He looked away from the conversation. He seemed to be bringing something in.

He talked about his devotion to the word of Christ. He was still as he spoke. His voice had an accent of gratitude to it. Tristan has a connection to his faith that could move mountains. The conviction in what he believes is going to touch the lives of many. And I am humbled to call him a friend.

I asked where his conviction came from. He answered by saying 'Jesus.' I asked him where the certainty of that is found. His response was no shock. What he said silenced my world, but it was no surprise. Tristan said that having faith in Christ is entirely about love. And embracing that, is about removing all hesitation. He said meeting faith with intent was the answer to all questions of doubt.

He steadied himself as he shifted forward in his seat. He looked at me directly. He said: 'You ask me where the conviction of love is found, and I return the question to you.' He didn't move as he waited for a response. I noticed him. I felt my eyes start to smile. I saw his relax.

I answered gently: 'Love comes from within; that is where it's found.' Tristan just sat back, took a deep breath and said with relief:

'As is the certainty of Christ.'

Friday

Understanding the importance of meaningful connections is about including yourself in what's found there. It's a gnarly paradox that's separated by nothing.

I can't engage in what makes life so amazing without including myself. And simply acknowledging that reminds me of how much has changed recently. There is no way I would have admitted that before now. But remembering to include yourself in the stories of your life is about understanding what you bring to them. It's less about self-gratification, and more about awareness. It's about self-awareness, and there are no gruff bits to that.

I did something new today.

I started the day thinking about which person I wanted to share it with. And quite surprisingly the answer was myself. When I think back to how I used to operate, I feel like I should whisper the writing of that. But the truth is, I wanted to treat myself to a little bit of Simon today. And so I did. I grabbed a book and went to my favourite bakery in Mount Lawley.

The first time I absolutely loved reading was about 20 years ago when I read *The Way of the Peaceful Warrior*. It was the first book I couldn't put down. Today I treated myself to it whilst eating some of my favourite food (which is bagels) and drinking some yummo coffee. To be honest, the whole idea of checking-in with myself gave everything a silent edge.

As I walked into the bakery, I felt steadfast and still. I sat down with a coffee, and immediately noticed a guy roughly my age sitting on the other side of the room. He acknowledged me with a slight nod, as he lifted the book he was reading. It was *The Power of Now* by Eckhart Tolle. He tilted his coffee in my direction and took a sip. I did the same whilst tapping my index finger on my book.

The guy smiled and said: 'Great minds hey…' I replied: 'With two really good books to keep us company I guess.' We politely laughed in agreement.

But I wasn't up for small talk. I focused on the intent of the moment. It had a compelling stillness to it. I felt strangely calm and awake. I was really enjoying the silence of my own company. And I was confident my body language was displaying every part of that.

After a while, I became aware of the guy across the room again. Without looking in his direction, I assumed he would be noticing how steady I was. He was probably picking up on my calm demeanour. In the end, I couldn't help but look over at him. He noticed almost immediately. I smiled, as I moved my eyes across the room. I said with a certain amount of confidence: 'It's the stillness right?'

He nodded without replying, but I could tell he got it. I knew he saw just how 'in the moment' I was. And that's basically when I confirmed it.

I went to take a sip of coffee, but I missed my mouth, and spilt half of the bloody thing down the front of me. The shock of it was also how I almost broke my tailbone after falling out of my chair. I sat fallen, holding my coffee-soaked shirt away from my skin. Instinctively, I looked up hoping for sympathy. The guy across the room gave me the thumbs up and called out directly:

'What you've got there is the stillness buddy!'

Saturday

Last night I was talking to Jess and Haylie about this dialogue. They asked about it during dinner. I mainly spoke about the past week. The girls seemed interested enough. They liked that I was catching up with so many different people. They certainly enjoyed yesterday's story.

Later in the night, I was tucking Haylie into bed. And before I go on, I remind myself that she's only 10 years old. I went to switch off the light before leaving her bedroom. She said 'Dad' like it was a question. I replied with the standard 'yes beautiful girl' as I turned around to see her face snuggling into her pillow. She yawned and said: 'Where's Pa?'

I had not seen my father (Peter) in quite a while. After Haylie's question, I noticed a feeling of restlessness about that. And these days, noticing those sorts of feelings is a showstopper. Consequently, today is when I acknowledge my Dad. Quite frankly, he is one of the greatest men I know.

I caught up with him today. Although we haven't touched base in a while, he greeted me as if the opposite was true. My father has an acceptance about life that's difficult to describe. It comes from a place of freedom. He allows others to walk their path, and find their own answers without any outward judgment. No matter what he faces, he meets life with a unique acceptance.

He is a master of accomplishments as well. He could walk amongst the kings of the world just as easily as he would play with a child in a treehouse. He is always ready to assist when needed. He pounces with generosity all of the time.

It was great to see him today.

We didn't really talk about anything too heavy. I didn't hit him up with any of the stuff that's been going on. It felt disingenuous to do so. However, as we talked, I realised something profoundly important. As Dad spoke, I saw Jess and Haylie within me. I saw the connection that comes with family. Realising that, I felt nothing but gratitude for the man he was.

Before leaving, I acknowledged just how much I appreciated him. I could see he understood. Then he said he had a favour to ask. Although it surprised me, I was ready to do whatever he needed. And I told him exactly that. He asked that I take my feeling of appreciation, and offer it as a gift to my children. I couldn't help but think about Haylie's question from last night.

Before I got into my car to leave, I told Dad that I would honour the girls as he wished. Although I meant what I said, it didn't feel like a significant moment. Honouring Jess and Haylie is one of the easiest things in the world.
As I opened my car door, I flippantly waved goodbye without looking back.

Dad called out: 'Do you know what sits beneath what I ask of you?' Without breaking stride, I yelled back that I didn't. He answered with one word…

'Immortality'

Instinctively, my head spun in his direction as soon as he said it. And in true Peter Moxham style, he just shut his front door as if it was a lazy Sunday morning.

I love him so much.

Sunday

And then there was Astrid.

A lazy Sunday morning is precisely what we had today. Astrid got back from working away yesterday. I've felt like a little kid in a candy store all weekend. I invited her over for a family lunch. She accepted, and I was pumped.

She's been talking to the girls on the phone often over the past couple of months. They're never long conversations, but they seem to sustain all of them. I'm thankful they keep in touch. Having Astrid over was breezy-lemon-squeezy. She mainly hung out with the girls and our little puppy. It was good to see everyone so relaxed together. To begin with, there was very little significance attached to the day.

However, Astrid mentioned something while we were doing the dishes together that almost made me drop a plate. Apparently she found an old diary that she started after moving to Australia. She came across it after unpacking some of her belongings. I didn't even know she was that way inclined. When I asked about it, Astrid said she hadn't written in it for years. Apparently, she started writing because she didn't know anyone over here. She found the dialogue comforting.

I could relate. I almost told her everything about this story. I noticed a feeling of nervousness in my stomach. I felt my chest rise as I went to tell her. But Astrid spoke before I could. She explained that after reading some of her diary, she understood why our relationship ended.

I thought I was going to explode.

Astrid reiterated I was never going to end us. She understood that for things to change, she needed to act. Through reading her diary, she saw the common thread of our demise. She said one of us needed to act on our unhappiness. And even though it broke her heart, she felt compelled to leave.

It was a lot to take-in after everything that's happened over the past couple of months. I didn't know how to respond; didn't know where to begin. Astrid laughed. She was amazed to see me speechless.

I went to respond several times. But all I could do was put my index finger and thumb together, and point them at her, as I made stupid little noises.
I spluttered out a series of ums and hissing sounds. I had the eloquence of morse code. I had to go into the bathroom and splash water on my face.

Eventually, I calmed down enough to speak coherently again. But the moment seemed to have passed. I didn't really see an opening to re-engage the conversation. I waited until Astrid was leaving. As we walked to her car, I explained that I understood exactly why we fell apart. And then, much to my surprise, I touched the side of her face gently. I told Astrid I intended to find her again.

Without flinching, she looked at me with her scientific eyes, and said quite analytically, 'Why so confident?'

I answered immediately: 'Because I acted upon our unhappiness as well.'

Monday

After yesterday, I've noticed feelings of excitement and doubt over what happened with Astrid. Part of me was pumped about it. But at the same time, I also had feelings of apprehension. I wondered if I was moving too fast for her. Neither reality mattered that much though. Feeling like that was a natural experience to have. I didn't become what I felt. I just went with it. My feelings had an undercurrent of authenticity.

I'm happy Astrid was part of this thing lately. I certainly don't need to ask what finding fulfilment means to her. Her story is an appropriate example of how faith in a higher purpose does not always require a label. She doesn't spend too much time questioning her faith. Ask Astrid to explain her connection with God and she will point outside. One of the ways she finds fulfilment is to be with nature. Her theory is if random-nothingness were the artist of life, then being out in nature wouldn't feel so amazing.

Hang on, I'll try to write her chain of logic.

She says if - an amoeba actually grew gills - followed by legs - which then led to the ability to walk upright - that eventually evolved into having opposable thumbs - then - life could look like anything.

Astrid says science cannot account for the beauty in life. Her story about God is an appropriate way to wrap up what I've been doing lately. Being out in nature is 'a calling' in Astrid's life. Of that, there is no doubt. And when she's out in nature, it is the connection with all things that sustains her. It's got nothing to do with the name of God.

It's entirely about a universal feeling of connection.

Tuesday

Sometimes it's about the wish you didn't know to make.

I thought it was time to move onto the next thing. I don't know why, it just seemed like the right time. My instincts were screaming at me to go back to the library today. Initially, I thought it must have been about the silence that is found there. But I was wrong.

As soon as I walked through the doors, I saw my mystery library companion from roughly two weeks ago. She was sitting in the same place. I panicked. I rushed straight over to her and blurted out, 'I've been writing about other people's expression of faith and fulfilment and I'm pretty sure you are meant to be part of it!'

I just stood there looking at her. I was breathing quite heavily. I could feel my heart beating in my chest. I suddenly realised I'd dropped half of my stuff on the way over to her. She quietly looked at the path behind me, and then motioned for me to have a seat. She called me the 'water guy.'

We spoke for hours. As it turns out, she's writing a book. She follows Hinduism, and wanted to write about her faith. Talking with her made me feel like a little kid. She was so confident and graceful with her words. She didn't seem to waste anything during our conversation. Everything she shared had a purpose, and all of it led somewhere.

I was left completely blank when we finished talking. I had absolutely nothing to offer the conversation. As this wonderful lady went to leave, she picked up a pen that I had dropped earlier. She threw it to me and said: 'Have you ever noticed how you can't help but follow your feet?'

I wish I had got her name.

Wednesday

A little over a week ago I set out to connect with others. I wanted to hear from the world. I wanted to feel the gift of sharing. To begin with, I felt a little concerned that doing so would take me away from the momentum of this dialogue. I wondered cautiously if catching up with others would detract from what's been going on.

And on that front, there was absolutely nothing to worry about. When you are willing to trust your instincts, with the certainty of a sunrise, there is nothing to worry about. If your intent starts from the things that connect us, the truth of our lives, then you will not stumble as you engage your insights.

The voice of my instincts has never been louder. My higher purpose has never been easier to recognise. And the reason is found in the stories of the people around me. It comes from the thread of life that brings us together. We all desire fulfilment in this world. The manner in which we reach that fulfilment may have different accents. The things we put our faith in might look different. But the deepest type of fulfilment does not.

We are all an expression of life. And we all have a reason for that. I've been talking about faith a lot lately. But I'm not just referring to a biblical type of faith. I'm talking about the actions to attain fulfilment. Without our ability to believe, there would be no way for life to know itself. Without faith, there would be no recognition of that.

That is the truth of our lives.

CHAPTER FOURTEEN

Gift of Freedom

'What we make matter in this world is simply a question of perspective. And the blank canvas to every moment allows us to add meaning to whatever we choose.'

Thursday

Okay then. That's interesting. I feel like shutting up for a bit. I'm a little tired of making everything so significant. I feel like eating chocolate instead of drinking herbal tea. Tonight I blow a big-fat raspberry to my insights. I will admit, there is something scratching at the back of my mind. There is a surprising truth to the ultimate reality of life. But for now, I blow a Bronx cheer at whatever it is. I want to not care for a little while. Let's be random.

Two weeks ago, I acknowledged starting this entire dialogue in the eighth month, August, of the year. The number eight represents the infinite nature of the universe. The symbol eight, placed sideways, represents infinity and perfection. Which are two words that could be used to describe God.

But originally August was not the eighth month of the year. In 45BCE, Julius Caesar introduced the Julian calendar. Under the previous Roman calendar, October was the eighth month of the year. The word October comes from the Latin Octo. And I'm going to have a little bit of fun with that tonight.

The Gregorian calendar is the one we use now. It came in to play in 1582. That was when we decided to add the months of January and February. Consequently, October went from being the eighth month to the tenth. Before that, the Roman calendar only had 10 months that spanned 304 days. Every month had either 30 or 31 days. There were roughly 60 days each year that were not represented on the calendar.

Now, I know next to nothing about numerology. My knowledge of it is matched by my interest in it. Mostly, the subject does not matter to me. However, I thought it might be fun to look into the significance of the number eight.

Check it out:

- In the language of mathematics the number eight (horizontally) is the symbol for perfection and infinity.
- In Hinduism it is the number for wealth and abundance.
- Which is similar to its meaning in numerology.
- In science the atomic number for oxygen is eight.

- The eighth teeth on either side of a person's mouth are called the wisdom teeth.
- The Book of Genesis indicates that God breathed Adam to life on the eighth day of creation.

According to the book of Genesis, God created people on the sixth day.

> 'Then God said - let us make people in our image, to be like ourselves. They will be masters over all life...'
> Genesis 1:26

It explains that it was on the eighth day that God breathed Adam to life. It's an interesting point when you consider the atomic number for oxygen. This is what was written after God rested on the seventh day:

> 'And the Lord God formed a man's body from the dust of the ground and breathed into it the breath of life. And the man became a living thing.'
> Genesis 2:7

So it would appear that humans from a Biblical sense took their first breath, on the very first eighth-day, during the first time we ever bothered to measure the thing we call time. I would imagine it was quite a moment for the number eight. Seems to be the birth of its significance.

The only thing I don't like about the number eight is that all spiders have eight legs. It's too many, and sometimes I feel like they are on me.

Friday

Being the scribe for others over the past couple of weeks has reminded me that life is a subjective thing. Yesterday's dialogue was an example of that. What we make matter in this world is a question of perspective. I used the significance of the number eight to illustrate that. I just added a little meaning to it. And the blank canvas to every moment allows us to add meaning to whatever we choose, whenever we choose.

In the spirit of that theory I shall keep going.

As it turns out 1989, for better or worse, was a massive year in the history of things that matter. It was the year that the World Wide Web (WWW) was created. A British engineer, Tim Berners-Lee was an employee of the European Organisation for Nuclear Research, better known nowadays by its French acronym CERN. He wrote a proposal for a more effective communication tool, known at the time as ENQUIRE. That communication tool eventually became the World Wide Web. 1989 was the beginning of all information being a simple click away. Berners-Lee is the reason the world has become a lot smaller.

In many ways, his work from nearly 30 years ago is part of the reason I keep up with this dialogue. It is through engaging in the things that matter to me that keeps this conversation going. From a certain perspective, looking into what has always fascinated me is why I continue to write. The World Wide Web certainly makes that process easier.

I have activated my life through looking into it. The other day, I found myself telling Jess and Haylie to disregard their distractions. I encouraged them to take up what matters the most. On a broader scale, I try to imagine what would happen if everyone did that. It could be this simple: if you want to know what matters, look into your life.

Saturday

Whenever you engage in things that matter, 'time' seems to slip away. Our perception of it is relative. I was awake into the early hours of the morning. I got somewhat lost reading up on different historical events. And it all started because Tim Berners-Lee wrote a proposal in 1989.

Actually, when I think about it, '89 was a big year for me. It was the first time I fell in love. It was the start of my first long-term relationship. I was a bit of a sports-nut back then as well. I played plenty of tennis when I was a teenager. I idolised Steffi Graf and John McEnroe. They were absolute legends of their time. I guess if someone were to read this dialogue, they would not realise just how much I enjoy sport. But truth be told, sport is one of my favourite things. I'm sure my neighbours could testify to that. I get quite rowdy watching it.

The Australian Open is my favourite Grand Slam event in tennis. Australia entered the world stage of tennis in 1905. That was the first year we hosted the Australian Open. 1905 was also the first time Australia had a Davis Cup team. The Australian Davis Cup teams represent the second-most successful tennis team in the recorded history of the sport. It is second only to the USA.

As it turns out, a lot of fun things happened in 1905.

- Australian tennis hit the international stage.
- The Australian Cricket Board for International Cricket was founded.
- The Chelsea Football Club was founded in London.
- Ty Cobb made his debut for the New York Highlanders. That team became the Yankees eight years later.
- Yankee Doodle was No. 1 on the US billboard for 14 weeks.
- The first icy pole creation was recorded. An 11-year-old boy, Frank Epperson, invented it after freezing a soft drink with a stick in it.
- Until 1905 a Coca Cola product, marketed as a tonic, had traces of cocaine in it (not sure if that was fun or not).
- The Daiquiri cocktail was invented in Cuba.
- The self-proclaimed Entertainment Capital of the World - Las Vegas - was established.

- Sterling Price Holloway, the original voice of Disney's *Winnie the Pooh*, was born.
- The first ever meeting of Rotary Club members took place in Chicago.

Phew!

I want to emphasise that I don't hold a special connection with that time in history. Everything I've just emphasised (my love for sport and the significant events of the past) is nothing more than an example of adding meaning to things.

I started out today by emphasising that time seems to slip away when you engage in what matters. Our perception of time depends on our focus. It is completely relative. And the point I am making to myself here is this: exactly the same thing can be said about adding meaning to your life. Whether life has any meaning is relative. It depends on what you make significant. Making something meaningful is an act of creation. Like everything in life, it comes from within.

Oh, and before I log off for the night, I should point something out. There is another event in 1905 that holds some significance. That was the year that Albert Einstein published his Special Theory of Relativity (followed 10 years later by his General Theory of Relativity).

> *'Before God we are relatively all equally wise and equally foolish.'*
> Albert Einstein

Sunday

I am not going to try to unpack Einstein's Theory of Relativity. I don't have the inclination to do so. And I have a feeling if I tried, I would have a collapse of cognitive consciousness or something.

I'll just say this: Einstein's theory basically proved that time and space are no different from each other. They are in fact spacetime. The quantifiable results from measuring time are relative to what is happening when it is measured. Einstein proved that the observation of time could look different for two individuals without either observer being wrong. The relativity of time is a quantifiable physical truth. It is a provable fact that it is a moving target.

Everything I've been talking about recently is about the relative nature of the world. More specifically, I have focused on what matters. But it hasn't been done for superficial reasons. It's been more about adding meaning to whatever you choose. And I shall continue with that theme for now.

I will deliberately take the physical truth behind the relativity of time, and put it into the metaphysical world of my story. I do not view time as a real thing. It resides in the intangible world of things we cannot see, touch or feel. It is found in the constructs of a person's mind. It reminds me about detaching from the potency of your thoughts. Recognising that you are more than your thoughts is very similar to seeing time as an intangible reality.

Our thoughts are a question of perception. Feelings start from the same place. What we make matter, in this relative world, also depends on what each of us has seen throughout life. Our thoughts and feelings change quite often. Our perception of time seems to change according all of those things as well.

Let's map it out:

- The essence of time cannot be touched. Nor can a person's thoughts.
- How time feels depends on how a person feels. Thoughts are subject to the same test.
- Time can distract all things. Lord knows our thoughts can as well.
- You cannot use the five senses to understand either of them.

- Time can be slowed down (time dilation). Thoughts can be slowed down (Satori).
- They can be the measure of success for those who are ruled by them.
- Time is not a straight line. Your thoughts are not on a straight-line continuum either.

Time and thoughts can make things easier from a certain prospective. They seem to slip away when you go after what matters in your life. The relative nature of all things is a simple case of perspective. Einstein, and many other really smart people, proved that to be the case. And because all of that is true, it means our fulfilment starts from nothing.

Monday

French philosopher and mathematician René Descartes famously said: 'I think therefore I am.'

I'm pretty sure that's about self-awareness. The idea being, if you know you think (if you are aware of that) then you are. Lately, I reckon it could be cleaner to say: 'I think therefore I'm missing it.' But who am I to declare such a thing I guess.

Descartes said this as well:

'Nothing comes from nothing'

On the surface, that quote seems to be a reflection of its own message. Meaning, nothing begets nothing. But everything I've been doing recently has led me away from that idea. The relative nature of life is found within. And it is a gift of freedom to anybody who understands it.

The ultimate reality to who we are comes from an expression of love. For that to be true, there can be no right or wrong found there. That is to say, love in the highest sense knows nothing of judgment. There is no right or wrong - good or bad - in the ultimate reality of life.

I'm not dismissing the idea that painful behaviours exist. I think it's wrong to say or do hurtful things. Nothing good can come from treating others poorly. I've never felt comfortable embracing that there is no such thing as 'wrong' or 'bad' behaviours in the world. I'm not here to throw tinsel over the tough times and pretend they don't exist. In this relative world, painful things happen. And I choose to face that with authenticity.

However at our deepest level I know, without having to ask anyone, that we are here to experience love. We are the expression and fulfilment of that. Life exists so that we may experience the connection we share with the world. It is less about rules and more about choice.

There is a type of stillness that blankets the world. It is a light that cannot be measured. It is from this stillness that we come to be. We are an expression of life, from the stillness of love.

And there is nothing beyond the choice of that reality.

Tuesday

Only through understanding what love is, can we see when it's missing.

Love knows nothing of sorrow. But that does not mean that sorrow doesn't exist. At the highest level, sorrow can reflect what's missing in order for us to act upon it. Recognising the smallness of things like sorrow, doubt and worry can be the trigger to changing those things.

And coming from that perspective, there is nothing wrong with sorrow, doubt and worry. Without them, in this relative world, we could not explore the depths of those feelings. Without the opposite existing, we would not have a place to start.

To understand that is to understand that ultimately there is nothing stopping us in life. Everything that is separate to the feeling of love exists so that we may explore who we really are. And that understanding reveals a surprising truth: ultimately there are no 'road rules' in life.

That's not to say that life is empty. I've never enjoyed hearing that life has no meaning. And I will not advocate that point of view. This is my story, and as long as my hands are responsible for the message, there will be nothing written about how life is empty and meaningless.

Life itself is what gives everything meaning. We live in a world of cause and effect. Understanding the responsibility of that makes every moment colourful. Recognising the purpose of your life is about influence. It's about seeing just how much influence you have. Not only in how your life is played out, but also with what matters to the people you touch.

Every moment in life is an opportunity to create something extraordinary. And it all starts from the blank canvas of stillness.

God is found in such places.

CHAPTER FIFTEEN

Voice From the Stillness

'It is the wonderment of the night sky that awakens the possibilities we face.'

Wednesday 6:25am *'Let's plant some trees.'*

That's what I woke up to this morning. As soon as I'd dropped the girls at school, I went straight over to my mother's place. We spent the day in her garden getting our hands dirty. Initially, we talked about arbitrary things. But it didn't take long for Mum to change that.

She was putting a baby tree in the ground. As we worked, she asked if I was paying attention to the process in front of me. I questioned if she was referring to our task for the day. Without looking up, she asked the question again.

Not knowing how to respond, I explained the past month with elaborate detail. Mum listened silently. She didn't stop working, but I knew she was listening to every word. As I unpacked what's been going on, I realised the enormity of everything. I glimpsed the endless possibilities of talking about God and the Creative Force of the Universe. I felt both overwhelmed and in awe of such a thing. Approaching the paradox of those two feelings left me in complete silence. My larynx seemed to be constricted with anticipation.

Mum simply looked to the heavens and said: 'And now we're finally talking!'

She immediately asked what I had to offer regarding the past month. She acknowledged the stories of others, and then asked what I had to say about it. But all I had was silent anticipation. Mum stood up slowly. It was almost as if she stopped working in order to look at me. She seemed to be addressing parts of my psyche that I didn't know about. Eventually her gaze narrowed gently to mine.

She said: 'It's time for you to remember. It's come to that now. Don't worry, the rest will follow.'

Thursday

Before I go any further I need to square off here. There is a French term that means 'the reason for existence.' Raison d'être. It represents 'the everything' in life. Raison d'être is the light of your soul. It is the thing that connects you to this experience. It represents the relative reason each of us experience life.

As I look to remember, I think back to a couple of weeks ago. I remember what it felt like to be the scribe of fulfilment and faith to those close to me. As I look back, I automatically reflect on a significant thing that happened. Something I didn't mention a fortnight ago.

Everything that I am came from this moment. It's the reason I can close my eyes and breathe in with gratitude and fulfilment. Something happened on a particular day, not so long ago, that is the reason I know God. It is the reason I have an awareness of self.

It was 63 years ago yesterday.

My mother Anne was born into this world. I have not seen a more potent wisdom than in her eyes. She has a poet's heart. She blankets life with light and energy. She is a reflection of love. Her life is an expression of the highest form of it. All that is written here is but an echo of what she brought to it.

Happy birthday Mum, today you are my raison d'être.

Friday

It's time to remember.

I have never questioned the existence of God. My first experience of Her gentle touch was enough to sustain me for life. I actually have no idea why I have not brought this up sooner. But as I remember, I start by retelling the story to myself. Strangely, it all started from a place of doubt and worry. In fact, it was the most profound sense of worry I've had. It feels weird to be talking about it now but evidently here goes.

It was at some point in the 1980s. Nicola, Jamie and I were spending the Christmas holidays with our Dad in Canberra. I can't remember the exact details, but it was an Australian summer when President Reagan internationally addressed the issue of increased tensions in the Cold War. I'm pretty sure it had something to do with the nuclear arms race.

As strange as it sounds, I remember freaking out when I saw Reagan's televised address. I remember feeling apocalyptic dread for some reason. I was silently convinced the world (my world) was doomed. I can't remember exactly what Reagan said, but it left me convinced that Armageddon was upon us. And I carried around the feeling of dread for months. I could not shake the feeling of impending doom. So great was my fear, I was unable to mention a word of it. I was too young to be able to rationalise what I was going through.

I remember feeling edgy one morning after we had returned from our holiday. I decided to go for a bike ride. I had a fleeting moment, where I actually thought the dread I felt was going to take hold forever. I was compelled to be outdoors and to stay on the move. Something happened that day that changed everything. It was about noon, on a humble little backstreet in South Perth, that my world changed forever.

Halfway through the ride, I remember asking myself if the doom I felt was going to consume me. I didn't expect an answer, so I asked the question with conviction. There was form of surrender in my voice.

As soon as I uttered the words everything stopped. The world went quiet. It was about midday, but it was as if time no longer existed. I had no idea what was happening. All I could do was look around. The only thing I was able to accomplish was to notice life.

From the stillness of my rhetorical question, I heard the clearest most convincing voice I have ever witnessed. I was encouraged to calm myself because everything was going to be okay. I actually can't describe what the voice sounded like. It was deafening-voiceless communication. It was a whisper of something. But it also had the strength of a sonic boom. What I heard could not be ignored, and yet it remained discreet.

But my experience did not end there.

As soon as I heard the voice from the stillness, a sense of peace washed over me like never before. I was comforted and embraced by an orchestra of wonder. The joy of the world seemed to fill my lungs. The relief I felt cannot be put into words. It was the first time I felt my eyes shine. I could literally feel the life in my bones. It felt like my soul had decided to have a turn.

Coming from that reality, I felt compelled to notice. In fact, I had become the very essence of awareness. Everything around me was alive from the inside out. By my waist, on the side of the path I was standing on, was the most vibrant pink bush I have ever seen. I could see the life rippling out of it. The pink-colour was oozing with energy. It looked like a cartoon to my young eyes. Somehow, the life in the plant was no different to the stillness everywhere around me.

Everything was part of the whole. The stillness was glowing with movement. It was all an expression of life. I was a witness to it, just as much as I was part of it. From the ripples of stillness, everything was the energy of love. It was all God. He was the creation of life, and the witness to it. Everything existed for no other purpose. And the light to all of it was eternal.

It was without measure.

Saturday

It was almost like my eyes snapped open when I woke today. I didn't just feel awake; I felt alive. I was conscious of every part of my body as it nestled into the comfort of my bed. The softness of the sheets felt no different to the calmness of my breath. I had no presence of thought. There were no questions to ask of myself.

My intention over the past month was to bring God into the conversation. It's become obvious that this dialogue is a huge part of the cultivation of my soul. And I was not going to go any further without moulding God into the lines of the story. I know, with the certainty of a sunrise, that what I'm writing here will be with me forever. It's something I will always have. And what I described yesterday could very well be the reason for that.

I started to feel slightly confused about how to wrap it up though. I didn't feel overly qualified to explain the nature of God in a simple page or two. Who am I to talk about such things? At least that's what the anticipation of it felt like.

But the truth is, any description of God is limited. God is everything. She is all of it. I see now that my problem wasn't about trying to encapsulate the meaning and purpose of God. My problem was I wanted to be right about it. That's what slowed me down here.

But now I get it. There is no right or wrong in this part of the conversation. The shaking-finger of 'I told you so' does not belong here. God is a never-ending process of creation. All of life is an expression of that.

And we are here to remember it.

Ripples *of* Stillness

Sunday

If this story were for others, I would have it be about relationships. It would be about unity and the things that connect us. As always, I simply got out of the way and allowed the lines of the past month to flow from nothing. And almost all of it was about the things that connect us.

Nothing in the ultimate reality of life is about division. We are not here to honour loneliness and suffering. We don't need to hide behind the smallness of doubt and worry. Quite obviously, sometimes these things are a part of the human experience. But that doesn't have to mean we here to honour them. Ultimately, the dark things of the world exist so we might recognise the light within.

One of the ways to conceptualise the feeling of that, is to be still and not ask questions of the world. The verbs of God start from a place of stillness. All of life ripples from there.

If this story were for others, I would emphasise this...

There's a light to the stillness of life.

Beyond the preoccupations of doubt and worry

there is a light that stretches to the horizon.

It pervades all things.

It resides in the quiet soul.

It is brought to life by this indelible truth.

Deep in the heart of us there is a light that

connects everyone to the only thing that has ever mattered.

Love.

Monday

I keep thinking back to the first time of things.

So many people question the existence of God because of the dark things in the world. Questioning the potency of God because there is suffering in life has always felt incomplete to me. It's like blaming yoghurt for having live-cultures in it. The process of life is an organic experience. It is the backdrop to our corporeal reality. We have made sure of that together.

We are not here to bathe in the absolutes of the universe. The process of life isn't about that. The way in which everything plays out is a question of perspective. It is entirely relative to all that has come before us. We have made sure of that together.

One of the things that connect all of us to this human experience is the need and want for fulfilment. But the highest form of that does not come from expecting only bliss and happiness from the world. The deepest form of fulfilment is not about eradicating pain and suffering. If those things did not exist, we would not be able to recognise the opposite. Everything exists for a reason. We have made sure of that together.

The universe and all life are part of a cosmic plan. There is a process at play. We are not here to execute the plan, or recognise the entirety of the process. We are here to create our experience of it. The deepest form of fulfilment comes from remembering that. It is about the realisation of self. All of life is God at play, and we are the colours of Her experience.

The paintbrush at the easel of life, is choice.

Tuesday

The highest form of fulfilment comes from self-actualising the experience of life. We are exploring the evolution of our lives here. Much like the light of God, we are doing this together in order to expand the light found within. The horizon of possibility we gaze at is not set in stone. The process of life is always expanding. The collective nature of the human experience is all part of that.

God is the energy of love. Everything that is found here expands from a place of stillness. The absolute of the universe is the stillness of God. It's all love, it's all the energy of love. Ultimately the expression of life, the movement of it, is simply the evolution of that.

The colours of love can be found in the silence of the morning sun. That is the peace we find there. The sound of dawn is the stillness of God, it is the whisper of anticipation against our cheek. It is the wonderment of the night sky that awakens the possibilities we face. The fragrance of nature is the scent of God's love. That is the gratitude we feel at the flowers of the world. God is the snow that rests peacefully on the mountaintop, so that we might know the strength of silence. The light blends through the darkness, so we can feel the warmth of hope in our bones. God is the energy of love, so that we might recognise that within.

The halls of faith are made from such things. The beauty and wonder of life comes from the faith of God's love for it. And the only way in which all that can be realised is through our experience.

We are the conceptualisation of God's experience.

Wednesday

If you want to wake up to the beauty of God's love then simply engage in life. To love life - is to love God.

C S Lewis said this:

'A man can no more diminish God's glory by refusing to worship Him than a lunatic can put out the sun by scribbling the word, 'darkness' on the walls...'

I don't know why, but when it comes to God, the term 'worship' seems out-dated to me. I think it has something to do with rules. I don't see God caring about the rules we make up. He is the ultimate observer of the universe. He is the stillness of love that we feel in our hearts. And it couldn't matter less what name we give that.

It's less about rules, and more about engagement. That's not to dismiss the idea of rules though. I'm not saying that the path to love is paved with cobblestones of anarchy. You are not going to find your way to a beautiful life by hurting others. You are not here to honour loneliness and suffering. But for me, that is less about worship and more about something else.

Your life requires commitment. But that does not mean that you will only find your way to worthiness if you follow certain man-made rules. It comes back to the first time of things. If you want to see the innocence of God's love, then watch a baby interact with life. If you feel it's missing within you, then pay attention to the children of the world.

We are not here to hurt each other. You are not here to be cruel to the world. If you are wondering how to have an experience of God, then know this: if what you are doing does not involve love, then you are not having an experience of God. Whatever it is that you are doing, if it doesn't involve the softness of love, then that is entirely on you.

God is love. We do the rest.

And never forget, love is constantly talking to you. The Creative Force of the Universe is always reaching out to you. It's found in the conversations you engage in - the things you keep thinking about. It's found in the silence of your insight, and in the movement of your words. Art will take you there. Music will sing to you about it.

Love is constantly trying to comfort you. Go for a slow walk, and notice the sweet scent of Mother Earth. She will show you the love in the world. Surely if God was a painter, the colours of nature would be on Her palette. And all of it is for you.

There's no parable to write today. I will not end the past month with a cute little story about God. I will simply say this. There is light in the stillness of love. And it is you.

PART FOUR

NOVEMBER

The Stillness of the Moment

CHAPTER SIXTEEN

What Next

'Once you see the stillness that shines through the world you will automatically feel the gentle touch of choice'

THE STILLNESS *of* THE MOMENT

Thursday 1 November

Trying to unpack the nature of God in a simple story is a bit like trying to explain the brilliance of Mozart with finger paint.

Moulding God into the lines of this dialogue was amazing. The intent of the past four weeks felt incredible. I've never felt closer to the people in my life. I also have a profound sense of who I am and what I stand for. The light of responsibility for my life has never been brighter. I've never felt more alive.

But I'm very aware that everything I have written about, and therefore experienced, is completely relative to the story of my life. I am not here to preach to the page. And I'm not here to dismiss the experience of others. There will be nothing written about why I am right, and that therefore someone else must be wrong.

The expression of a person's faith doesn't have to be about proving something wrong. Dismissing someone else's beliefs so you feel better about your own is not faith. You cannot meet the fulfilment of your life on a field of doubt and worry. If you question your life from a baseline of doubt, then you are just adding that to your experience. You are simply fortifying doubt by backing it in.

The depth to faith is about intent. The clarity of what you believe is made stronger with conviction, not competition. Rather than seeking to make others wrong, this story seems to be about the opposite. And although I have absolutely no idea what that looks like…

I move forward to find out.

Friday

I have never felt a deep connection of fulfilment and love, without first feeling a type of stillness within.

Three months ago I started this process because I was sick and tired of what I've always done. I engaged in this dialogue because I was fed-up with the routine in my life. I assumed all of this was a simple conversation with myself. In a lot of ways, this dialogue is like a hidden camera. It is verbal surveillance from behind the counter of my insights.

Which is to say, I have been communicating with myself from a place of certainty. I've been addressing the silent parts of my world. And I have held absolutely nothing back because there's been no reason to. It's quite a thing to explore the silence of your inner world without needing to check with anyone. I don't think it's necessarily about speaking from the heart though. It's more about speaking directly to it.

Originally, I assumed I was communicating from some kind of baseline of silence. It was about taking the movement of my words, and putting them on the stillness of a blank page. I thought this dialogue was about speaking from the anticipation of silence. It was about coming from nothing. And in many respects, that remains the case. But at the same time there is something else going on - and it can't be ignored anymore.

It is somewhat incomplete to say I'm speaking from a place of silence. Every time I've felt a profound sense of anything good, it has come from a comforting type of stillness. But that doesn't mean I'm simply communicating from that reality.

It's more like the stillness is speaking to me.

THE STILLNESS *of* THE MOMENT

Saturday

I felt quite strange today.

I might not be here to preach to the page, but it sure feels like I have been lately. I guess it's not necessarily a bad thing. I've just felt a little too lofty of late. And a good way to put a stop to that is to wake abruptly because of a bad dream. I keep having a weird dream that's difficult to describe. So for now I'm not going to try.

I felt slightly on edge today. It's nothing major, nothing to worry about. I've just had a sense that something strange is going on.

There are some major differences in my life now. The values I hold, and my general behaviour have changed considerably. I no longer feel the need to react impulsively to every little problem that comes up. I no longer feel the need to create drama in my life.

But that's not to say every moment, in every day, is full of celestial fun and happiness. I have no desire for things to be entirely about dance floors and disco balls. I'm happy to meet the difficult times with authenticity. And sometimes that requires critical thinking, and a willingness to leave certain things alone. It's not always about reacting impulsively to things.

It all comes down to observation.

Not so long ago, I became what I felt too often. If I was angry and impatient, I expressed it as if I was a victim. The most frustrating times were when I thought people didn't listen to me. In fact, I spent so much of my life thinking that nobody noticed me. And I was more than happy to play out the frustration of that.

My life seemed to be nothing more than a reaction to something. The difficult times were kept alive through my behaviour. I was in a constant state of emotional self-defence. The tough times were reinforced by what I brought to them. My behaviour fortified what I was going through. And there was actually part of me that loved it. I revelled in the drama.

I'll slow down a little bit here to highlight something important. What I just pointed out has nothing to do with what was wrong with me. I haven't acknowledged all of that to beat myself up. My behaviour in the past was not wrong. It is more precise to say it was small. I was keeping my life small because the opposite felt too risky.

But I realise now that my feelings, whatever they are, don't need to define the day. They don't need to be the inevitability of my behaviour. I can simply recognise the authenticity of them. I can choose to see the so-called negative times as a natural part of life. Rather than reacting impulsively, I can use them as a springboard of possibility.

And that's how the small things become something more.

The Stillness *of* the Moment

Sunday

Again with the strange stuff.

Tristan surprised me somewhat when he came over today. Obviously, it wasn't strange to see him. But the manner in which he showed up, and what he asked was a little weird. We have known each other for almost 20 years. We can go weeks without any contact, and then catch up without missing a beat.

It's his instincts and sincerity that are so easy to like. His passion for life is quite infectious. Every time we talk, the day feels bigger and brighter. I always feel more awake after spending time with Tristan. He is completely spontaneous. Yet, you always know what you are going to get with him. It's both somehow.

But today he did something I'm not sure he's ever done before. He certainly hasn't done it with me until now. He just showed up out of the blue. He rocked up unannounced, and he seemed more serious than usual. All of that sounds quite insignificant as I write it. But Tristan never shows up without warning. It quite simply has never happened before.

As soon as I opened my front door, he explained that we needed to talk. He walked in without waiting for a response. I started to feel nervous. But he quickly reassured me that everything was okay. Nothing sinister had happened or anything.

Tristan had spent the morning at church. He said he didn't enjoy the service because he was too distracted. For the past three months, he had been trying to find a way to get me to join him there. Given everything that's happened recently, he thought I might find comfort in the support of his church community.

Initially, I wondered if he showed up unannounced to try to recruit me. But what he said next was somewhat surprising. He said that after the church service he knew he had to come straight over. He reiterated that he has been waiting for the right time to talk to me about renewing my Christian faith. But then he realised he didn't need to. He followed up with a question I didn't expect.

He asked me to explain why he didn't need to.

I found myself talking a lot without saying much. Tristan, being who he is, just kept interrupting with the same question. Everything about the situation eventually sharpened my awareness. I noticed a heightened sense of things again. Without making a big production of it, I settled myself and then spoke from there.

I told him everything. I left nothing out. I shared more openly about the past three months than I have with anyone else. The conversation was not a verbal mugging though. We unpacked everything gently and with purpose. We did it together. The whole thing was like one big jam-session.

I found myself talking about meditation more than I would have anticipated. It was virtually impossible to refer to the fulfilment of the past couple of months without mentioning it several times. I couldn't stop talking about the peace that is found there. Tristan asked what it felt like. In the end, he wondered if the reason he came over was to find out.

As soon as he asked the question, I shot up from my seat. I walked straight over to an open window and gazed out at nothing in particular. I spoke without thinking: 'It feels like forever.'

Monday

No matter the question, meditation is the answer.

If someone is ready to wake up to life, meditation could be the how of it. The act of meditating regularly is the key at the doorway of self-awareness. In fact, that's what it means to be a Buddha. It is not a reference to just one man in history. Buddha refers to anyone who has woken up to the truth of life. It refers to someone who sees the true nature of things.

I've dabbled in meditation throughout the years. I have always been drawn to the idea. But I can't say I took it on with any kind of real commitment until just recently. Initially, I was meditating every day because I felt profoundly broken. The hurt I felt when Astrid and I spilt actually scared me. It seemed too deep. Every part of me was drenched by it.

I knew that what I was going through required more than just a band-aid. It wasn't something I could ignore. There was no running from it. The hurt I felt needed to be addressed. I had to face it softly. And meditation was the answer.

It reminds me of something American author Neale Donald Walsch wrote…

'If you don't go within you go without'

To me, that sums it up perfectly. If you don't look within, it doesn't really matter what you find. It's all about insight. It's totally about exploring your instincts from a backdrop of silence. There is no limit to the potential for your life if you are willing to interact with the silence of the world. If you are willing to notice that, to explore it without restriction, you will automatically wake up.

And like most things with any kind of spiritual journey, there are many ways in which that can be accomplished. It's not about learning the one true way or finding a secret to something. Self-awareness is not found in the back-alleys of the world. It can't be ordered on-line. You can't scroll through it on your phone. It's not necessarily about instant self-gratification.

It's a human experience, and therefore it doesn't look just one particular way for everyone. The softness of meditation is devoid of any kind of harsh rules. It doesn't require any elbow grease.

But it is a commitment. It takes a certain level of engagement. Sometimes you'll have to roll up your emotional sleeves and get stuck in. There's a vulnerability that comes with meditation that requires something from you. There are some gentle questions you will have to ask yourself. But having asked, you will be answered.

The Stillness *of* the Moment

Tuesday

The softness of meditation doesn't have any harsh rules.

The way in which someone can connect with the stillness in life is virtually limitless. Just like the depths of a person's imagination, the possibilities are infinite. Meditation is simply an activity. It is a passive one. It's all about being still. But it is an activity nonetheless. And it is the archway to connecting to the silence of your inner world.

Meditating is about stepping aside from your distractions. If you can notice the clutter of your thoughts without reacting to them, you will have unlocked something. You will have woken to a new possibility. Meditation is about becoming mindful of who you are.

It's about being mindful of the moment. If you can practise that from time to time, you will ease into a type of peace without corners. It will be something you can relax into during difficult times. Being mindful can help you remain calm even when the outside world is coming at you with the opposite.
It becomes something that's going on, rather than who you are.

The stillness of meditation and mindfulness is about observation. You don't have to be what you think and feel all of the time. It is about seeing the choice of things. You don't have to play out every emotion if it does not serve your best interests.

We all have a type of stillness within. And we all have the choice about going after it. It comes down to how you want to share with the world. And you can't address that question without becoming aware that you have a choice about the answer.

Ripples *of* Stillness

Wednesday

You are not your behaviour.

You are completely responsible for it. Each of us is responsible for how we act in life. We might not always do that consciously and with poise. But the responsibility of how we act with certain things cannot be outsourced. It comes from within. At the deepest level, and when referring to emotions, nothing happens to us.

The other day Haylie got really excited after one of her favourite songs came on the radio. She turned it up and said: 'I love this song. It always makes me happy.' Now my little girl is only 10. She is not finished emotionally cooking yet. I don't expect her to have the wisdom of the Dalai Lama.

But at the deepest level, what she claimed is impossible. Haylie's happiness is not at the whim of something. A song, or anything else for that matter, cannot make someone happy. Happiness can come as a result of something, but that doesn't mean it rocks up randomly to surprise people. It doesn't mean it happens to you.

Happiness comes from within. It's a unique creation that sits within each of us. To explain, I'll ask myself this: If Haylie's favourite song had magical powers, and could make people happy, then how does it pick and choose who gets to experience that. I wonder what magical potion they used in the chorus to make that possible.

Obviously songs don't pick and choose who gets to be happy. We do. We choose our individual response to things. Just because sometimes it's done spontaneously, doesn't mean it happens to us. In Haylie's case, she chose to like the song. Her feelings about it were a result of something. They are a result of her collective experience to this point. The song isn't responsible for her happiness. It can't make her feel anything.

Everything I am pointing out is about becoming conscious of your life. I'm talking about waking up. It's got very little to do with someone's favourite song, or a magic potion to something. I'm talking about the potency of our behaviour.

The Stillness *of* the Moment

How you behave has a profound effect on how others relate to you. Your behaviour can determine the accent of your experience. That's certainly the case with the outside world. Which is to say, people are going to behave in accordance with your behaviour. They will act on what you show them. But none of that means you are the definition of those things. It's more precise to say you are the choice of them.

And if you are wondering how to explore that, then just be still. Find a way to go within, and touch the silence that is found there. Once you have woken up to it, simply notice.

Ripples of Stillness

Thursday

I needed to get out of the house today.

Things have felt a little too wordy for me lately. I think it's because I miss Astrid a little. I haven't seen her for a while. Apparently her job is really busy at the moment. And I've been in my head too much with all of that.

So I decided it was time for some fresh air. I went to one of our favourite parks around the corner. It's a beautiful place. It has a quiet little pond in the middle. The pond is surrounded by heaps of wise old trees. They seem to shield the water from the wind. It is always completely still. And that's how I feel every time I look at it.

I meditated at the park for quite a while this morning. I sat against a tree and then just slipped into the sounds of nature. The more you connect with the stillness in life, the easier it becomes to see it everywhere. With practice, you can tap into it whenever you want. It's just like reading a good book. You can pick up where you left off without any effort.

I left my MacBook and all of my writing notes at home. I wanted a break. I'm glad I took my phone though. I've got a few meditation tracks I listen to whenever my head gets too busy. Guided meditation can help when you feel too distracted to do it by yourself. But I didn't end up using the tracks today. That wasn't why I was glad I had my phone with me. Nicola called just before I was about to head home. It was good to hear from her.

We had a brief chat about things. We talked about normal brother/sister stuff I guess. At the end of the call, Nic asked if I'm still on track with everything. She asked about Astrid. She also questioned if I've been getting out enough. I explained where I was, and filled her in as much as I could. She queried the tone of my voice. She thought I sounded a little flat. Although I understood why she mentioned it, I didn't have the energy to unpack everything completely.

I said there was nothing major to worry about. I told her about all of the meditation stuff, and how good it feels to connect with stillness and peace of it. I mentioned that my baseline thoughts and feelings were quite settled at the moment. But I reiterated that I've also felt a little strange lately. Without being able to explain, I said it felt like I was missing something. That there was something I wasn't picking up on.

And what Nicola said next just added to the weirdness. She acknowledged that being out in nature was a good thing. She liked that I was at one of my favourite spots. But then she randomly asked if I had bothered to take off my shoes and go for a walk there.

I have to admit, I was a little too abrupt with my response. We swore at each other for a while. And then she urged me (whilst laughing) to give it a go. I explained that I would try it later. But for now, I was going home to eat ice cream. Nic asked what flavour. I told her cookies and cream.

She said she was heading straight over.

Friday

It's easy to assume stuff.

Until recently, I assumed anything to do with spirituality was mostly for hippies. I had this picture in my head that said if you meditate all of the time, you'd probably end up wearing orange pyjamas and shaving your head. I thought that sort of stuff was for the monks of the world.

It's amazing to see how many times I didn't try something new because of my assumptions. I would picture that a situation was a certain way, and then judge it without knowing anything about it. Not only would I do that sort of thing out of avoidance, I'd happily crap on about it as if I was an expert.

My life at the moment is a perfect illustration of what I'm talking about. I recognise there's a strong spiritual theme to what's going on. And although I didn't set out for that to be the case, I absolutely love it. I've never felt more content. I have never been more purpose-driven. Even when things are a little off, I still feel completely excited about life.

But none of that means I am acting like some kind of pious holy-man. I'm no Jedi. Taking on a spiritual thing doesn't have to mean filling your world with herbal tea and incense. It's not about conforming to any kind of stereotype. It's an individual thing. And it has absolutely nothing to do with being perfect.

I meditate a lot. But I still get bogged-down and confused sometimes. I have connected with the stillness in life. But I still trip over the furniture every now and then. I am content. But I still feel unhappy from time to time. I can look at things with soft eyes now. But that's only because I can see the harsh times clearly.

THE STILLNESS *of* THE MOMENT

Saturday

I was meant to meet Astrid in Fremantle today. We planned to have lunch somewhere on the cappuccino strip. But she cancelled first thing this morning. Apparently something came up at the last minute. I decided to go by myself anyway. Fremantle has a cultural feel about it that you won't find anywhere else in Western Australia.

I had been looking forward to going all week, and I wasn't missing out because Astrid pulled the pin. I ate some beautiful street-side seafood paella after wandering around the markets there for most of the morning. Everything was completely relaxed. It was great to breathe the sea air for a while.

However, coming from the relaxed atmosphere of everything around me, I noticed just how tired I felt. My body was heavy and fatigued. It reminded me of the fast-paced nature of things lately. Everything has been quite full on. Not in a bad way though. There's nothing manic about the past couple of months. It's just that I've been super engaged in things. I spend no time sitting around waiting for life any more. I no longer lay on the couch avoiding stuff. Every day is full of purpose and action.

But as great as all of that is, I actually felt quite whipped today. It was like my body didn't want to keep up any more. I decided to get a massage. I went to a quaint little place in the central hub of Fremantle. If a person can't detach whilst getting a massage then I'm not sure they ever will. It felt so good to just chill out and slow everything down.

Initially, I imagined it'd be a great way to end my day out. But as I was putting my shoes back on (after the massage) I remembered what Nicola said a couple of days ago. She suggested I walk barefoot in nature for a while. As soon as I remembered, I felt a surge of spontaneity. I went straight down to the beach.

Mostly, I just walked along the shore for a while. Nicola was on to something. The feel of the earth under my feet was very soothing. I guess it's no big thing to walk barefoot. But to notice it with every step, with every movement you make, is an amazing thing. The crunch of the sand between my toes took me back to something. I felt little. I remembered what it felt like to play with nature. I remembered the adventure and innocence of it.

As my body moved, the earth beneath me did as well. I stopped for a moment to look at the calmness of the ocean. I felt the same within. I walked into the shallows of the water and stood quietly as the current splashed around my ankles.

I had become as steady as everything around me. I had connected with the stillness of the moment again. I was basking in the silence of nature without asking anything of it. My awareness stretched out like the horizon before me. I took a deep breath out of gratitude. It felt like I was exploring a miracle.

The ocean started to pull against my ankles. I looked down as the tide began heading out. From the stillness of gratitude, I felt the immeasurable force of nature at my feet. It has strength like no other.

It reminded me of my Dad.

The Stillness *of* the Moment

Sunday

We spent the day in his workshop.

I rocked up to Dad's place to find him building a doll's house. The man is always doing some kind of woodwork project in his spare time. He's never happier than when he's making something for his grandchildren.

It's been exactly four weeks and one day since we saw each other. I walked into the silence of his workshop and watched him go at it for a while. He was completely focused on what he was doing. You could almost smell the poise and concentration in the room. Eventually my gaze caught his eye. Dad just looked up and said: 'Oh good. Come on then, let's get on with it.'

We worked in silence for most of the day. I don't know why, but the whole thing felt like a cathartic break from the story of my life. Somehow, everything that mattered didn't for a while.

Eventually, I asked Dad about his passion for woodwork. I wondered where it came from. He talked about his late father for a while. Without stopping, he spun his finger in the air, and explained that everything around us was handed down to him. He loved making things with his hands, because he always felt close to his father when doing so. He also explained that the workshop felt like an emotional safe haven from everyday life. Dad used his time there to detach from things.

What he said next brought me to this page tonight. I haven't told him anything about this dialogue. But nevertheless, Dad said that making things out of wood is a form of meditation for him.

As soon as he said it, my eyes immediately shot in his direction. I watched him sanding down a piece of wood. He worked slowly. His focus was precise. He held the wood in the air, and looked down the surface of it. He whispered with one eye closed, almost like he wasn't even talking to me. He said softly: 'And there's no limit to it.'

At any other time I probably would have freaked out. But nothing really surprises me any more. There is still part of me that can't comprehend why

Dad brought up meditation. In the face of everything I've been talking about, I just can't understand the apparent coincidence of it. And no matter how deeply I look, I can't find the answer. But I also don't care that much either.

I guess it's not for me to know at this stage. There are some things in life that don't need to be explained. I know for a fact there are no coincidences in life. But on the other hand, I've no idea why providence is full of surprises sometimes. I guess I'm not here to know everything there is to know. And on that front, I thank God out loud.

I am however, compelled to acknowledge what Dad said. I won't let the moment pass without embracing what happened. And he is spot on. There is no limit to the way in which you can connect with the stillness of life.

Meditation isn't entirely about sitting quietly with your legs crossed. It doesn't always have to be about breathing calmly with your eyes closed. It's not necessarily about tuning out. Meditation is about being mindful of the moment. And the how of it is limitless. The stillness of life doesn't discriminate. It sits within each of us.

Rather than tuning out, it's entirely about tuning in.

The Stillness *of* the Moment

Monday

It's about becoming conscious of your life.

To explain, I will talk about something I brought up at the beginning of the month. I remember saying I used to go through life thinking that no one listened to me. I was convinced that nobody noticed me. It was something I constantly told myself. And I completely trusted what I believed. I saw it as the truth of my experience.

It was a lonely existence, but one I revelled in somewhat. I used what I told myself as an excuse to be apathetic and disengaged with life. Every time I came across an emotional roadblock, I would just roll my eyes and be critical of whoever caused it.

There was very little responsibility in my life because I wasn't conscious of it. I was way too busy pointing the finger at my discontent. But that wasn't always the biggest problem I faced with it. My biggest problem was I believed what I was telling myself. I trusted that I was right.

And here is the point.

Being mindful of your life is about choice. I cannot say that enough when talking about the stillness of the moment. One of the first things you will find from the silence of your inner world is the choice you have about how your life unfolds. You will see the noise of your thoughts as part of the experience, rather than the entirety of it.

You are not the tough times you face. You are not the doubt that comes with that. You are the choice of those things. It's about what serves your best interests. It all comes down to being self-aware. If you can find a way to wake up, you can choose to compartmentalise your discontent and have a shot at everything else.

You get to be anything.

Tuesday

I'm constantly looking to engage with the world lately.

I woke up this morning feeling completely charged. I couldn't get out of the house quick enough. After taking the kids to school, I had breakfast at our local café. Initially, I planned to spend the day outdoors. I wanted to chill in nature. But I'm pleased to report, none of that happened.

While I was eating brekkie, I heard a familiar voice from behind me: 'I thought you might be here.' I turned to see Astrid smiling at me.

Apparently she had the day off because she's flying out with work tomorrow. She was heading over to my place when she saw my car at the café. So she joined me for breakfast. And I say 'yay' to that.

We ended up spending the first part of the morning together. The two of us have always enjoyed people-watching. It's a non-intrusive, silent thing we've always done together. It's interesting watching people interact with the day. That's mainly what we did together this morning.

Astrid and I are talking regularly these days. More often than not, we keep in touch with texts and emails. We've also been talking on the phone regularly. But it was great to actually spend time with her today.

After a lot of not talking, Astrid leaned over to say something. But she was interrupted in the weirdest way. An elderly gentleman walked straight up to our table. Without any clear reason he started talking about his grandchildren. He pulled out photos of his family and started gushing over them. Initially, I thought he might be a little bit crazy or something. I shifted in my seat uncomfortably and started searching for whoever was meant to be looking after him. But then something changed.

This guy was not crazy. And he had something to say. Within a matter of seconds he sat down with us. I guess in the past, I would've done something to stop what was happening. But hearing this big jolly man was encouraging. He spoke so passionately about his family. It was difficult to ignore. He was not ranting though. He was just a grateful grandfather, passionately talking from his heart. I heard my father in his words.

THE STILLNESS *of* THE MOMENT

Towards the end of our conversation, he looked at me and said: 'You've figured it out haven't you?' I could feel Astrid staring at me. I asked what he meant without needing to. He looked around the room and said: 'You've worked out the most important part of this whole thing.'

Looking down at my hands, I quietly agreed I was starting to. The man immediately slapped the table and laughed. He leaned over and grabbed Astrid by the wrist. He shook her hand in the air. It was almost as if my answer was a celebration to this stranger.

As he was walking off he turned around. With a huge smile on his face, he said: 'And you share it with others?' He looked at Astrid. I nodded with a smile that matched his. He walked away laughing.

After he was gone, Astrid remarked in a very thick German accent: 'Jesus, Maria und Joseph. What in God's name just happened there!' She said she hasn't seen anything quite so strange before.

I leaned over and said with anticipation: 'Now let me ask, did you feel something surge at all?' She just threw her hands in the air and yelled: 'What the hell is everyone talking about!'

Evidently, not so much with the surging thing for Astrid I guess.

Check that.

Wednesday

I wish Astrid wasn't working away again. Apparently it's a short trip this time. But I'm still a little bummed-out about it. We haven't seen each other much lately. We talk most days, but I miss hanging out with her. Sometimes I wonder where the two of us are heading. Most of the time I just compartmentalise that stuff. What will happen between us is going to unfold over time. I'm not wasting too much energy trying to predict the outcome.

I trust my life these days.

It all comes back to the theme of the past two weeks. I am not living out the uncertainty of Astrid and my future. I'm not stressing about it. I see the choice in what I tell myself now. Rather than becoming what I think and feel about the situation, I am embracing the stillness that sits behind it.

I am playing out the stillness of my life with intent. It's not entirely about coming from what is found there though. It's more precise to say that you are in a partnership with the stillness of life. It's cleaner to acknowledge that you are dancing with the silence of your inner world. We are the verb to the stillness of the moment. We are the movement that is found there.

And there is no limit to how someone can tap into that. It awaits all of us. It isn't something to find, the stillness is there to be remembered. The possibilities of how to remember are limitless. You simply need to look into your life. And once you have noticed the peace that is found there, something amazing will happen.

So will others.

The Stillness *of* the Moment

Thursday

It's entirely about observation.

Noticing the stillness in life is about seeing it within. It's a reflection of something that isn't always immediately obvious. You cannot touch the stillness of life without recognising the movement that is found there. You can't explore one without understanding the other.

Everything that exists comes from the never ending expansion of life. We are the movement of that. All that we experience is a creation of it. We are a reflection of the life we see. And there is no place that reality doesn't exist. There is no scenario where it does not apply.

The 'what next' of it is choice.

Once you see the stillness that shines through the world, you will automatically feel the gentle touch of choice. It's everywhere. The peace that is found in the observation of life is not entirely about surrender and inaction. It's more about connecting with the endless possibilities that come before you.

At the deepest level, there is nothing in the stillness of the moment without our experience of it. The whole thing is an interaction of the highest order. However, it is incomplete to say that we are here to reach the stillness and peace of the world. That sounds more like a goal setting exercise. The stillness of life is not just something to hope for one day. It's more than that.

It's about the choice of things. Understanding the potency of what is being said here is about action. The stillness in life is not there to be reached. It exists to be welcomed. It is something you enter through self-awareness and inner-reflection. The stillness that shines through the world has always been there. It's an indelible everlasting part of life that can never be tampered with. It has a voice.

And you are it.

CHAPTER SEVENTEEN

The Certainty of a Still Heart

'Being genuine is the substance and structure in faith'

The Stillness *of* the Moment

Friday

I tried out one of my theories this morning.

I've said that no matter the question, meditation is the answer. Well, Jess asked what was for breakfast today and I blurted out 'meditation!' She just looked at me as if I had hit my head on something. So we had cereal instead.

I love Jess and Haylie so much. I can't declare that to the universe too often. I can't remind myself enough. They teach me so much. They show me the importance of not taking things too seriously.

Not everything in life needs to be overly significant in order for it to be important. Not everything that matters needs to be raved about. That's not to confuse anything. There's nothing wrong with noticing the significance of something. But it doesn't mean we have to run around sticking a flag in everything.

Rhetorically speaking, if you can't laugh at your life then what the hell are we doing here. At the deepest level, happiness is a choice. So are all other emotions as well. Quite often, it genuinely feels like things happen to us in life. And in many respects, it is that way. But at the deepest level, our emotions do not happen to us. All feelings can be a natural part of the human experience.

But none of that has to be slowed down by the weight of significance. I remember saying recently that I hardly recognise the person I see in the mirror any more. And a major reason for that is because I've lightened up considerably. It would seem that when you start waking up to the potential for your life, you automatically stop taking yourself so seriously.

It's about replacing significance with sincerity.

Saturday

The potency of what someone believes is about sincerity.

Being genuine is the substance and structure in faith. One of the quickest ways to dilute doubt is to be sincere with the world. I have already said that if someone can find their way to the stillness in life they will have unlocked something new. That's absolutely true. And what is found there does not discriminate.

The certainty of a still heart is a gift to every living soul. One of the ways to have an experience of that is to be sincere with the world. It is a sharing of something. To notice the stillness in life is one thing. That's enough. There is no obligation beyond that reality. There are no questions that come with it.

All of it is enough. But to interact with the certainty of a still heart is an entirely different thing altogether. If you act upon it, you will bring movement to the stillness of your life. You will take the knowing of something, and transform it into an experience.

It all comes down to being genuine.

When I address all of that, I recognise something compelling. And the anticipation of it has me shifting in my seat. I feel a little edgy as I look to write about it. But the truth is, there is no way not to be genuine as your life plays out.

You cannot find your way to being sincere. In many respects, it's a huge paradox. And it feels like I need to be a little careful as I explain it to myself. On the surface, it looks like the sincerity of our experience is met with two impossible realities. Two opposite contradictions meet to form a whole.

From the stillness of life, from the choice of that, I recognise that it is possible to be sincerely insincere. There is such a thing as being honestly dishonest. A person has the capacity to be genuinely fake as they go through life. It all comes down to how a person wants to share with the world. It's about what sort of life you want to lead.

Said simply, we are constantly acting in accordance to our beliefs. We are always playing out that reality. It is an unstoppable force. The experience of our lives is an expression of that. And it's entirely about being genuine no matter what happens.

We are the creation of our beliefs, no matter what.

Sunday

And I believe I'm a little dizzy after yesterday.

There are plenty of paradoxes at play. There's a real paradoxical feel to some of this dialogue. And the reason for that is quite simple. There is also a strong paradoxical theme to my life at the moment. I'm not here to talk about hard and fast rules. I'm not engaging in this thing to find the one true meaning to life.

It's incomplete to assume life is always about one particular thing. I am not looking for the illusion of that. I'm also not here to prove anything to anyone. It's got nothing to do with validating my point of view. What I believe has nothing to do with making others wrong. It is a flimsy thing to strike down another person's beliefs in order to reinforce your own. I'm not here to explore that stuff. I don't write to make others wrong.

In my world, exploring a so-called contradiction is exciting stuff. Meeting that which seems impossible is the beginning stages of all kinds of fun. I'm never more determined than when I'm told something can't be done. I never get more charged about a thing, than when someone else's expectations try to limit my own. I won't be stopped by contradictions here. I'm not slowing down for doubt.

However, none of that means every day is full of flowers and sweet smelling stuff. The idea of acceptance isn't always about shrugging your shoulders. You don't have to constantly submit to the needs of others for the sake of peace. Accepting different ideas and values isn't about being a wimp. That sort of thing is apathetic. Broad thinking has nothing to do with not caring. It's entirely about engagement.

And sometimes it makes me a little dizzy.

Monday

I caught up with Bryce today.

The past month seems to have flown by. The fast-paced nature of things has ramped up significantly. And I have absolutely no idea why. In fact, there's a real accent of uncertainty about my life at the moment. I haven't been sleeping that well.

But most of the time, I'm leaving myself alone with that stuff. I'm not adding too much to the uncertainty I feel. Rather than crowding it, I'm being patient. I am confident if there is something that needs to be addressed, it will eventually show itself. What will be will be. But having said that, I've felt a little tired of late. It feels like I've been drifting off course. Almost like I've been in my head a bit too much.

And that's why I caught up with Bryce today. In many respects, he's a lot different to Tristan. Each is passionately engaged with life. They have a strong sense of self. They are caring and genuine. But Bryce is a little more grounded and level headed than Tristan and me.

Often, if you can't find something within yourself, look for it in others.

Coming from the uncertainty I've felt, I knew it was time to check in with Bryce. He always reminds me to be steady and calm no matter what's happening. It's never about what he is teaching me though. He is not here to educate. That would be a tiring friendship. It's about what he shows me. It's about who he is naturally. Bryce is authentically calm and steady no matter what he faces. And through spending time with him, he shares that naturally.

We didn't talk about anything too heavy today. There was nothing overly significant about the catch up. It was good to just hang out. Life is so uncomplicated if you are willing to simply notice. And it was great to notice Bryce today.

And he said as much without me needing to. He acknowledged that engaging with others is sometimes a natural pick-me-up. He talked about measuring the influence of a friend by how you feel after hanging out with one. Bryce finished by acknowledging our friendship. Without making a big deal out of it, he said he appreciated it.

And the point he was trying to make was reinforced by what he shared. His generosity gave everything a real boost. I didn't feel tired after hanging out with him. He was so open and honest. I naturally wanted to return that to him.

In a lot of ways Bryce is spot on. The potency of a friendship can be reinforced by how you feel after spending time with someone. The measure of it can be about influence. And if you can't find that within, look for it in others.

The Stillness *of* the Moment

Tuesday

I couldn't stop thinking about something I mentioned yesterday.

I acknowledged that Tristan and Bryce have strong senses of self. It occurs to me that everyone I'm hanging out with lately is the same. Including yours truly. I am surrounded by people who have a strong sense of faith about who they are. And once again, I will stipulate that I am not only referring to a biblical type of faith when I say that.

I'm talking about the everyday type of faith all people have. I'm referring to what makes us tick. Who you are and what you stand for is entirely brought about by your beliefs. It is the faith you put in a thing that brings it to life. It's your beliefs that make it happen. And at the deepest level, it can't be stopped.

Even if you don't act upon something you believe to be true, it is still part of your belief system. Inaction about a certain thing doesn't mean stopping it. Let's pretend I don't like the careless drivers on our roads. Let's say I believe they are annoying and unsafe. Coming from what I believe, it would be easy to act impatiently when I'm driving. I could honk my horn and swear at these careless people in order to feel better.

And of the surface, you would think I could stop all of that by not doing it. I could simply ignore the urge to honk and swear.

But none of that is about stopping my beliefs. Even if you don't act upon what you believe, it's still part of your experience. We are always acting in accordance to our beliefs. That is the expression of our lives. Inaction is simply part of that expression. If I believe something, but do nothing about it, I am not stopping anything. I'm just responding differently.

It is faith that brings things to life. And the edge of that is sharpened by sincerity. Look to be genuine. Find what works and go after it. Other people can't answer these things for you. You have to go within and explore the silence of your inner-world.

Do it without checking with others, and you will begin to share yourself authentically. Not checking with others has nothing to do with arrogance though. It's not about shunning the people in your life. It's about exploring who you are so that you can share yourself consciously. If you look into your life, you will start to get a strong sense of self. And rather than shunning others, you will be moving closer to them.

As you begin to wake up, so will they. And you will be able to relax at the end of each day knowing you were generous and giving. Before you go to sleep each night you can close your eyes, and say these two simple words to the universe.

Yours truly.

THE STILLNESS *of* THE MOMENT

Wednesday

Man I miss Astrid.

It's been on my mind too much. Apparently she's back in a couple of days which is great. I hope we spend a little more time together soon. The lack of contact is understandable though. Spring and summer are the busy periods with her work. Astrid is always flying off to remote areas to survey different endangered animals at this time of year. I do miss her though. I'm looking forward to seeing her again.

I spent most of the day with Nic today. I wanted to get busy in the face of what I felt. But unlike times in the past, I don't intend to unpack everything we talked about. I'm not writing tonight to explain that. It was just good to hang out with my sister for a while.

I did a lot of the talking today. I couldn't stop referring to the theme of the past few days. I kept talking about potency of being sincere with the world. Nic was in a reflective mood. She seemed happy to go with the flow. Spending time with her reminded me about the importance of unpacking stuff.

Being sincere is the substance and structure in faith. The confusion that typically comes with doubt is completely over-shadowed by the strength of sincerity. And the deeper you go into that, the less you will care about pushing it onto others.

Self-awareness comes with an amazing type of confidence. It is soft yet determined. It is about relaxing into who you are without necessarily annoying people. There's no need to whack people with your emotional resume all the time. Not if you are comfortable within your own skin. Not if you are conscious of every part of that.

I'm never more drained than when someone is constantly talking about his or her achievements. I always feel emotionally gaunt whenever I'm bombarded with someone's internal resume. I don't say that to be harsh. And I'm not here to make others wrong. But it's just exhausting sometimes.

I don't mind if someone is a little insecure with life. It's not about that. I just get a little tired when a conversation is completely centred on how much someone knows. And I get particularly revved-up when others try to hide their insecurities behind a veil of wisdom.

That stuff is the complete opposite to being sincere. The search for constant reassurance is nothing in comparison to being authentic. The first reality is about wishing for something, and hoping people notice. The other is about unashamed honesty, and a humble desire to be generous.

The deeper I look into the stillness of my life, the more authentic I want to be. It's not about being better or more equipped than others. It's got nothing to do with being the tallest guy in the room. And it certainly has nothing to do with hiding your insecurities behind a barrage of waffle. That stuff is about not wanting to be vulnerable.

And being authentic is about the complete opposite.

The Stillness *of* the Moment

Thursday

For the purpose of this conversation, I will point out two different things. Solely for the purpose of what's going on here, let's pretend there are two different types of vulnerabilities.

The first type is not much fun. There is a type of vulnerability that you need to be cautious of. There's a shrinking, almost scary type of vulnerability that does not always serve you. A good example, without going to extremes, is the pain that comes when you stub your toe. Whack your toe on the corner of something and you'll feel the sort of vulnerability I'm talking about.

It's the type of thing that causes pain and suffering. That type of vulnerability does not always need to be embraced. It's found in toothaches and car accidents. It shows up in violent moments and in deeply sad ones. It's the unexpected break-in or the illness that takes us there. It is a type of thing that has us shrink.

But there is also a gentle supple type of vulnerability in the world. There is a type of vulnerability that allows us to expand and explore with unrestricted freedom. It is about sharing and generosity. There is a light within you that involves a gentle type of surrender.

There is a type of vulnerability in life that awaits your warm embrace. Who you are, your authentic-self, does not need to be hidden from the world. You cannot hoard the vulnerability that comes with self-awareness.

Behind the awareness of self, there is an infinite source of love and warmth. It expands beyond the measure of time. It cannot be restricted because it is a sharing of something. It cannot shrink because it never stops growing.

It is who you are.

CHAPTER EIGHTEEN

You Promise

'The only way the creation of all things can know itself is through your experience of it.'

Friday

It's late and I can't sleep.

I guess sometimes there are certain things that need to be addressed no matter what. There are times when you simply need to hunker down and face something. My life as I write about it, has nothing to do with avoidance. Waking up to the potential for your life involves facing whatever comes up.

It's not always about doing what's easy. Sometimes it's about addressing the things that aren't. If you want to live with purpose, if you want to be conscious of that process, then sometimes you will need to face things that will take you away from happiness.

And I say all of that because of a dream I keep having. This morning was about the eighth time recently that I've woken abruptly because of the same dream. It's difficult to explain. And it's not something I thought I had to. But it's obvious I need to find out what's going on.

So here goes.

The dream takes place under the night sky. It's a nocturnal thing. I find myself walking through a dense of forest of trees and rocks. At first, it's the silence that grabs my attention. It's cold there. The sound of the earth under my feet disturbs the peace. I walk through the darkness with caution.

The mist of heat from my breath evaporates against the silence of the night. I feel uneasy. It feels like I should whisper my breathing. There is a strange type of distance in the air. At first, it appears to be my only comfort.

But then I hear a voice.

It's a little boy singing in the distance. He is singing a Brooke Fraser song that normally brings me comfort in the waking world. It's a song about faith. And as quick as a thought is formed, I rush directly to it. It's instinct that drives me there. But everything slows down when I reach the little boy. My vision narrows to his song.

He looks past me though. His eyes glow bright like two stars that have become aware of their own wonder. He sounds like a little angel. He sings without music. His voice needs none. His face is glowing bright with life. It seems to darken everything around me.

I whisper the question: 'Is this real?'

The little boy stops. He warns me with the silence of his gaze. I am unable to move. I can no longer feel anything. The boy looks down at the ground. He stares at something behind him. He does not utter a sound. Something is coming.

I hear the deep roar of the world coming towards us. It is a guttural sound that's beyond comparison. I hear the earth being sucked into a void of nothingness. The ground starts to shake. The trees start to scream. And from the behind the still blue eyes of the little boy before me, I see a tidal wave rushing towards us. Its movement blankets the night-sky. The massive wave starts to crash in around me.

And I wake gasping for air.

Quite frankly, it's a dream I could do without. And all of a sudden I'm left wondering why I needed to unpack the whole thing just before bedtime.

I think I need a coffee.

Saturday

What will be will be, I guess.

I don't say that to be apathetic. I'm simply acknowledging that if there is something you need to address, life will find a way to make it happen. It's incomplete to assume words are the only way to realisation. Becoming self-aware isn't about controlling the medium.

It's about accepting whatever pops up in your life. Whether something brings you happiness or pain is not the point. Self-awareness is about knowing who you are no matter what you face. Acceptance has nothing to do with not caring though. It's about seeing the broad picture.

And sometimes seeing the broad picture is about remembering we don't always have complete control over everything. I remember back to the 6th of September. I listed some of my superstitions. I remember all the rules I had in my head. It feels great to loosen my grip on life. Clinging to the routine of your life has nothing to do with having control over it though.

Someone might do things in order to feel safe. But that does not mean that they have complete control over everything. I don't say all of that to invalidate the idea of having structure and routine. Sometimes those things can help you find yourself.

But that's different to always controlling stuff. Sometimes things are going to happen that you didn't expect. There will be times when you need to face something you would rather do without.

There is no potency, no substance and strength, found in constantly trying to chase down the easy things in life. Sometimes you'll need to unpack what is hard. And if you continually try to avoid that stuff, life will find a way to track you down.

Ripples *of* Stillness

Sunday

Astrid is leaving me.

Again. I have never found it more difficult to stick to my commitment with this dialogue. The only reason I am writing now is because I'm profoundly lost. I'm hiding here tonight.

Whenever I've considered the idea of getting back with Astrid, I instantly start to worry about losing her again. I didn't want to go through that sort of pain again. I certainly didn't want that for Jess and Haylie either. But it seems I've lost her without ever reconnecting with her in the first place. And it's all because I promised.

We had a little game we used to play. If there was something important one of us needed to say, we would start the conversation by saying 'you promise.' That meant the other person was obliged to listen without interrupting. You weren't allowed to speak until the other person had completely finished.

Astrid got back from working away yesterday. She asked if we could meet. We agreed to meet at the park with the pond. I thought we were catching up because we haven't had much contact recently. I was wrong. And I didn't anticipate what was about to happen.

I rocked up to the park a little early. I wanted to soak it all in before Astrid got there. I was sitting on a grassy bank watching the stillness of the pond for a short while. Then I heard Astrid walk up behind me. Without turning around, I greeted her. She sat down, looked at me with concern and said: 'You promise?'

I felt uneasy. I nodded silently as I looked down at the grass in front of me. Astrid spoke for about 10 minutes. She said she was happy for Jess, Haylie and me. She thought the three of us seemed closer and more relaxed. She talked a lot about our breakup. She had been trying to find her feet with the whole thing.

She started to cry gently. She said I seemed more relaxed than I used to be. She acknowledged that I had changed considerably. And she felt genuinely happy about that. She took great comfort knowing I was okay now.

The Stillness *of* the Moment

I was waiting for the punch line. And then it came. Astrid said that she was unable to find her feet with our breakup. She said that in many ways, my family was the only thing keeping her in Perth. She never intended to stay here for as long as she had. That's when she told me she was going back to Germany.

She couldn't say when. But she's looking at flights in January. She said she needed to be with her family. She planned to go back indefinitely. She wanted to clear her head and get a fresh start.

I felt my eyes giving in. I started pulling out blades of grass in front of me. Astrid rested her hand on top of mine. She said: 'Simon I have to do this.' And then she got up and walked away. All I could hear was the sound of her leaving.

I whispered gently: 'My heart, I think I'm writing my heart to you.'

I felt like a little boy. I wanted to disappear. And then a tidal wave of sadness roared over the top of me. Tears flooded my soul.

It was finally over.

Monday

That which I never had is gone.

Nicola came over today. I told her what happened, and she rushed right over. She seemed more heart-broken than me. I asked if she thought I should contact Astrid. I questioned if I should try to change her mind. Nicola said she had already spoken to Astrid on the phone. And there was no going back.

I just don't understand how this happened. I feel like an imposter in my own skin. For all my so-called wisdom, here I find myself. I feel completely blindsided. I sit here day after day and engage in a dialogue with myself. I come here for clarity and yet I have none now.

I rambled nonstop today. It must have been quite tiring for Nic. She allowed me to off-load without interruption. She was so patient. As I was talking, I became aware of how manic I was being. I didn't care though. I wasn't calming down for anyone. It was clear that I was in shock. It was obvious I was in a free-fall without a parachute.

As I sit here tonight writing these words, I feel quite confused about the whole process. I mean, what am I actually doing here…

Before Nic left she looked at me with determination and said: 'You know it was never about Astrid.' I blurted out that it was entirely about her. I clapped my hands out of anger and yelled that everything I've been doing was for her. I knew it was a lie.

But I simply don't care.

The Stillness *of* the Moment

Tuesday

I woke this morning to someone knocking on my front door. I sprung out of bed in a panic. I thought it might have been Astrid. I flung the door open to see Mum looking down at her feet. She looked up at my tired panicked state and said: 'And you were hoping for a happy ending.'

I rolled my eyes and went back to my bedroom. I yelled that I wasn't in the mood. I flopped down on my bed and starred at the ceiling with indignation. Mum stood in the doorway of my bedroom. After a considerable silence she said: 'Take me to this park of yours.'

I went to argue with her, but I knew we'd end up going anyway. I couldn't be bothered wasting energy arguing over the inevitable. I cleaned myself up and took her to the park. We went to the exact spot where Astrid and I sat together two days ago. I stood over the divot I had made from pulling out the grass. It felt like I had returned to the scene of a crime.

I didn't like being back there one bit. Mum explained she had spoken to Nicola. She asked if I meant what I said yesterday. She questioned if I actually thought everything that I'd been going through was for Astrid. She asked if this dialogue and everything else was about winning her back.

I said that part of me felt like that. Mum spoke without hesitation. She said: 'And yet you also see the absurdity of that.' I nodded in agreement. But I also challenged her without needing to. I asked what was wrong with hoping that Astrid and I would reconnect. I looked to the heavens and screamed: 'What's wrong with wanting that!'

Mum gently touched the centre of my chest. Then she cupped her hands over my temples. I impatiently asked what she was doing. She told me to be quiet. It wasn't a question. Almost immediately I felt completely relaxed. Everything started to slow down. It was like her touch brought on a waking meditation. We stood in complete silence for a brief moment.

Mum eventually told me to sit down. We sat together quietly for roughly half an hour. I soaked in the beauty and grace of nature's sweet touch. I also silently unpacked the past month. I had a wordless conversation with myself.

I was completely and utterly present. I had entered a state of absolute stillness.

I saw the events of the past couple of days as something that happened, rather than who I was. From the stillness of the moment, I detached from the drama of it. I saw that nothing actually happened to me. Astrid telling me that she is leaving was obviously an event that happened. But it didn't happen to me. I detached from the drama of the whole thing by remembering that I was the only one making it dramatic.

From the stillness of the moment, a state of complete awareness, I saw the story of my life. I recognised the responsibility I have in the things I tell myself. I glimpsed the infinite nature of unrestricted self-awareness. I saw the connection we all share.

I was so swept up by the experience; I almost didn't notice Mum walking away. I watched her quietly. She turned, and glanced at the sky. She shrugged gently and said: 'And that's not even the most extraordinary thing.'

THE STILLNESS *of* THE MOMENT

Wednesday

I lay in bed this morning with my eyes wide open.

I felt completely awake. I was thinking about Astrid. After everything that's been going on, I understood why she had decided to go back to Germany. I saw that ultimately, her journey had nothing to do with my expectations. She was not a trophy. And I'm not on a conquest here.

I don't have the appropriate words to describe just how quickly the past month has flown by. It feels like it all happened in a week. I have felt completely at peace - and entirely swept up by the action and adventure of the whole thing.

I didn't really know what to expect when I opened the dialogue for November. I didn't know how to top the feeling that came with talking about God.

But as it turns out, I wasn't done with that topic anyway. I'm not on a conquest with this thing. It's the process of self-awareness that brought me here. I have been exploring the stillness of the moment. I've been talking about waking up.

There is an everlasting type of stillness in life that can never be tampered with. It is the point of all creation. It is from this stillness, that everything comes to be. Life is a never-ending process of movement and expansion. And there's no way for that to be the case without an indelible type of stillness pervading all things. That is God at play.

And we are the experience of all of it. The only way the creation of all things can know itself is through our experience of it. We are the eyes and ears of existence. We are the realisation of that.

To conceptualise the creation of all things is to be self-aware.

Thursday

I meditated for quite a while this morning. The more you connect with the stillness of your inner world, the easier it becomes to see everywhere else. Everything that life has to offer is a reflection of what you bring to it. And the key to unlocking that indelible truth is insight. We are the eyes and ears of existence. But that's not just a physical reality. It's a spiritual one as well.

If you can find a way to notice that, you will see something amazing. The stillness of the moment is saturated by a horizon of light. It blankets the world you see even if you are blind to it. It is the beginning of all forms of creation. And no human heart can change that.

Life is a creation from the stillness of the universe.

And we are all part of the evolution of that. The universe, and all that life has to offer, comes from our collective experience of it. Life exists for the purpose of growth. And we are here to give it a voice. All of it is about the realisation of self. From the moment life exploded into life, we have been moving towards self-awareness. We are evolving so that the universe might have a concept of itself.

This is something 20th Century philosopher Alan Watts said about it:

> *'What you do, is what the whole universe is doing at the place you call here and now.'*

> *You are something that the whole universe is doing, in the same way that a wave is something the whole ocean is doing.'*

We are the realisation of the universe. There can be no 'here and now' without us. There can be no concept of life without our conceptualisation of it. We are the movement from the stillness. We are the creation of the life we see.

And when you move into that reality, so does the universe.

Friday

Well what a month.

Part of me feels like I tripped through a doorway. I find myself here after a whirlwind of something that's difficult to describe. The fast-paced nature of stuff has been quite full-on. Not all of it was that much fun either. But I take a great deal of comfort knowing that everything has happened for a reason. I know that it was all meant to be.

Sometimes you can't manipulate the world. Sometimes you have to find the strength to go on even if it hurts. Life needs texture. It has grooves and swirls to it. There are going to be moments of happiness, and times of sadness. There will be times of confusion. But ultimately, they only exist for the sake of clarity.

A life without chapters is a life without growth.

And none of it is about what's wrong with the world. The growth of your soul has nothing to do with being right, or better than anyone else. Waking up to your potential has nothing to do with achievements. It's not about reaching a certain destination. It's not about riding off into the sunset of victory.

There's nothing to win here except the realisation that you are enough. It's enough that you are here. There are no obligations beyond that. You are here to experience life. You exist as a point of creation.

And you are a sharing of this world. You exist so the creation of all things can know itself through your eyes. There is no other way for the Creative Force of the Universe to know what it feels like to be you. And there is no one else who can offer the sharing of that gift.

The destination of your life is in the here and now. It always has been. And life awaits your remembrance of that. There is no distance between you and your greatest potential. It is found in the certainty of a still heart. To be self-aware, is to feel the breath of God against your cheek.

Try to imagine you are a small part of a huge thing. And your fragrance of faith is why you are here.

Ripples *of* Stillness

Take yourself to the smallest flower in the greenest field.

Picture the tiniest little flower sitting quietly in the middle of a huge meadow. All this little flower knew of the world was the comfort of silence. It basked in the stillness of life. It imagined no other thing.

Until one day, the wind decided to blow gently against its little petals. The smallest flutter rang out across the silence of the meadow.

'Hello little one' whispered the wind ever so gently.

'Whoa!' cried the little flower, 'I didn't know I sounded like that. What's the how come of it?' the flower said whilst tripping over its words.

'We did it together' the wind said with joy, 'I am that which carries the all-of-everything. I am the gentle touch of the smallest whisper. And I am the almighty force of the loudest roar. And I have come to be with you.'

The little flower felt a swirl of excitement. 'Why have you stopped to talk to me? I am just a tiny little thing.'

'Well I have come, that you might see the opposite' said the wind.

'But how can you make me see?'

'My beautiful little angel, I am not here to show you. I have come to share with you. I cannot move through everything without moving through you. Your presence is part of the all-of-everything.'

The little flower fluttered once more 'But that means I'm not so tiny after all.'

The wind stopped completely. It spoke from a place of complete silence. 'No little one, you are part of all of it. Everything that is would be incomplete without your scent.'

'And your fragrance is shaping the world.'

PART FIVE

December

You

CHAPTER NINETEEN

Acceptance of Self

'You will find something deeper than happiness if you can accept whatever comes up in your life'

Saturday

I have come this far because of something I've never really had before. It's the complete acceptance of who I am and what I stand for. To be self-aware is to get to a place of complete acceptance. And I say that after being quite shocked by something I don't really want to acknowledge.

I realised something this morning that I did not expect. All of this is coming to an end now. I started this conversation with no view of where it was taking me. It was despair that had me start writing. The 1st of August 2012 will be etched in my memory forever. It was the day I started one of the most incredible experiences of my life. It was from despair, that I found the complete opposite.

Initially, I wrote so that I had something to do. I was looking for retrospective certainty. I used this dialogue to find clarity. One of the many things that has sustained me over the past 122 days is that I've had no agenda. I've just been going with the flow.

I never really stopped to consider why I was writing every day. The feeling I got when doing it was enough. I've never really questioned the process beyond that. And it never occurred to me that it would all come to an end one day. It's not like I imagined that I would write every day for the rest of my life. I didn't expect this to go on forever. But I also didn't put any thought into when it would finish.

Until today.

From the moment this dialogue kicked off, it has been about following my instincts. I have given my insights room to explore stuff. I do not have a set routine or a specific time I come here each day. I write when my instincts tell me to. And the content of this book has come from exactly the same place. I have simply been following my feet with this story. And this morning I instinctively knew something.

It's time to drop the hammer on this thing.

Sunday

Part of me wonders if it's because of Astrid.

This dialogue and everything I have been going through was not about winning her back. I understand that completely. I just wonder if there's a subconscious link between ending this, and Astrid going back to Germany. There's something logical about that idea. It seems like the right reason to finish what I started here.

It hurts to think about Astrid leaving. I find it tough to acknowledge. But I realise I haven't lost anything either. The fact is, I lost Astrid before she moved out. And there's no going back. I'm sad that she's leaving, but I don't feel heartbroken about it. I guess I've already mourned the loss of our relationship. I also understand where she is coming from. Astrid has reached a point where she needs to be around her family. And given everything that's happened, it is completely understandable.

I also take comfort in knowing that it was all meant to be. Everything that happened was for a reason. It's not for me to question it. What Astrid needs to do next has absolutely nothing to do with my expectations. I can't demand anything from her. It would be selfish to try to push her into something she doesn't want to do.

I also won't allow what's happening to derail my life. I am worthy of more than the struggles I have faced. Every person walking the planet is bigger than the struggles they face. It completely and utterly sucks that Astrid and I aren't getting back together. And that's okay. It's meant to hurt.

I can't imagine what it would feel like to not care about her. So I'm okay with feeling sad because she is leaving. I guess sometimes you've got to get out of the way, and allow certain things to download. It's about acceptance.

Astrid is leaving pretty soon. And I can't think of a better reason for this dialogue to end. I started writing when she left. And I will stop when she is gone.

Monday

I've finally arrived at a place of complete acceptance. And none of it means I'm always happy. I'm reminded of the depths to happiness every time I watch our little puppy jump around at meal times. Sometimes happiness is flimsy. There's nothing wrong with wanting to be happy. Like most people, I want that as often as possible. But quite often, it is only surface deep.

I have mentioned several times that I have no interest in my life being about the constant pursuit of happiness. And the most important part to highlight about that is the *constant* search for it. I categorically reject the idea that we're entitled to complete happiness all the time. That's nothing more than vanity run amok. Expecting that sort of thing reeks of a selfish type of entitlement.

Living with gratitude will create amazing things in your life. And expecting nothing but happiness is an ungrateful way to be. It is a profoundly incomplete expectation. And wishing for it quite often just produces the opposite feeling anyway. So many people are impatient with their lives because they measure everything against happiness. So many things are left incomplete because of it.

It's the idea of this rickety thing: 'If something or someone doesn't make you happy in life, then drop it and move on.'

And to that, I stick out my tongue and blow. You don't need to treat your life like it's a 24-month interest-free loan. Life is not always about instant self-gratification. The world isn't here for you to stick your hand out and demand stuff.

Sometimes I wonder if there are too many fair-weather friends in the world. I'm not specifically talking about my own life. I'm referring to all of us. So many of us have lost sight of our own resilience. It seems we don't want to explore the tough times any more. We push that stuff away. We seem to go after what makes us happy no matter what. And in doing so, we automatically dismiss the only thing that can get us there - the complete acceptance of self.

Tuesday

Whoa pull out the placards Simon!

I got a little revved up last night. I almost started ranting. I even went to slam my laptop shut after talking about resilience. I got a bit too excited for my own good. It was deflating that no one else is in the room here. I was a little bit flat because there was no one to high-five.

And there is something about that which needs to be addressed. Something has become apparent about this story, and it needs to be acknowledged. But I'll do it later. I don't want to change tack just yet. I'm going to stick with what I've been talking about for now.

It is somewhat flippant for me to say we have lost sight of our resilience. I don't say that to put others down. I'm not trying to be a human starting gun. I recognise that for every back that has been turned, there is always someone standing with arms wide open. There are so many people in the world who are here to help.

And it would be unfair to suggest that all people everywhere have given up on their own resilience. I do not advocate that point of view. I realise there are some real tough nuts out there.

But having said that, I stick by everything I wrote yesterday. It's not about belittling people. I don't write to make others wrong. Every line of this thing has come from my experience. I'm simply sharing myself. But none of that means I am the king of the castle. My experiences do not outweigh someone else's. I'm clear about all of that.

And I say what I'm about to with absolute confidence. Always striving to be happy is the very thing that prevents you from experiencing it in the first place. It is an expectation that has caused way too many problems in the world. Beneath that flimsy idea, there is something much more potent to be found.

Wednesday

There is very little difference between having self-awareness and being completely at peace with yourself. And in the face of that, happiness is not even the tip of the iceberg. It is merely a scattering of snowflakes over it. The expectation of constant happiness does not even register when talking about acceptance.

If you can accept whatever comes up in your life, you'll find something deeper than happiness. You will find fulfilment. And it's a rich experience full of substance and texture. It's not something to cling to. The fulfilment of your life does not need to be fleeting.

It has a depth that overshadows the expectation of happiness. And there is no limit to how someone can experience it. It is found in the really big things. And just as much in the small stuff as well.

It is everywhere. The fulfilment of your life could be as simple as coming home to your family at the end of the day. It could be found in the arms of someone you've missed for way too long. It's in the tears and laughter of the things that move us.

Your fulfilment awaits you. It can show up anywhere. The fragrance of nature might take you there. It could be in the scent of a flower, or the smell of the ocean air. It could be in the chapels and churches of the world. You might find it in the job you've always wanted; the thing you finally finished; the place you always go.

How we experience the fulfilment of our lives is relative. It can show up in countless ways. There is nothing to get right about it. There's no mandate you have to follow. It's about waking up to your life. Becoming conscious of your own fulfilment is about understanding one simple thing…

You are worthy of every bit of it.

Thursday

I've really been beating up on happiness lately. And the poor little thing probably doesn't deserve it. But I have to admit that I've felt happy doing it. Often the best kind of laughter is the one you bring on yourself. It's fun to laugh at your own jokes.

But in all honesty, I don't want to be flippant. Happiness is great. I absolutely love it. In fact, life would be excruciating without it. I'm not here to dismiss happiness with a whole heap of philosophical jive. Being happy completely rocks, and there is nothing wrong with wanting that.

But, just as the fulfillment of your life can show up in many different ways, the constant search for happiness can do the same. And it can cause huge problems. The expectation of happiness breaks up so many relationships. It starts all kinds of unnecessary conflicts. Wanting only happiness in your life can be heartbreaking. And normally we are too quick to point the finger when we are heartbroken. In fact, quite often it pollutes how we treat the people we love the most.

A lack of happiness can make us quit things too easily. For that matter, it can get us fired sometimes too. We buy stuff we don't need in order to find it. We will even move house because we think it might be in a different suburb. Often, we push ourselves to the point of exhaustion to avoid not having it. We even do exactly the same thing when it goes missing. And too often, we sit around waiting for happiness to show up.

The whole thing is a puppet show. But none of it is about beating up on happiness. It's the constant search for any kind of feeling that takes us away from the responsibility of our lives. The want for fulfillment is inherent in all of us. But that does not mean we should expect it all of the time.

Life is not always about just one thing. We can't always afford to be single-minded. We find ourselves here after an immense process of emotional-evolution. And we are the collective experience of all of it.

Friday

It comes back to something I mentioned about Astrid.

I said that I couldn't imagine what it would feel like not to care about her. And it's true for everyone else I'm close to as well. I think about Jess and Haylie. I don't ever want to know what it feels like not to care about them. Even just writing about it makes me uncomfortable.

And someone could quite rightly argue that it's reasonable to drop the things that make us uncomfortable. On the surface, it seems fair to want to run away from the tough times we face. It seems reasonable to distract yourself from that stuff. Perhaps that's why we're always looking down at our phones these days. So many people are not willing to look into their life any more.

Things are moving pretty fast. We don't seem to have much time for the gradual things. And there is no way we're slowing down for the unpleasant stuff. If something is trying to drag us down, we will sweep it off our coat-tails and keep moving forward. And it's all because we measure too many things against happiness.

But expecting only bliss from the world is an incomplete thing to go after. At the deepest level, eradicating sadness would mean the end of happiness as well. If we eliminate the need to cry, we wouldn't be able to recognise when to laugh.

I return to the thing about Astrid. The only way I could feel apathetic about her leaving, would be if I didn't care about her any more. I'd have to not love her. And loving Astrid is one of the greatest joys of my life. I have no need to distract myself from the hurt I feel about her leaving. Rather than trying to push the hurt away, I consciously allow it to download. I actually want to acknowledge it because I choose to love her.

And that's what it means to embrace acceptance. It's got nothing to do with going after happiness. In fact, it's not about going after anything. It's about owning your life.

Saturday

Mum sent me an email today. She said that she's been 'checking' my energy levels lately. I have no idea what that means. But I feel comforted by it anyway. She mentioned that she's picking up on certain things about me that I haven't shown her before. She liked the direction I'm taking my life at the moment. And in true Anne Moxham style, she ended her email with something Mark Twain said.

'The worst loneliness is to not be comfortable with yourself.'

She always seems to hit the mark. She always knows when to show up. Everything Mum wrote was quite different and a little surprising. She's like that sometimes. I was not shocked by any of it. I would not be where I find myself today without her. Sometimes I get quite overwhelmed by her generosity. I don't know how I will ever be able to thank her.

The Mark Twain quote is fitting. I don't feel lonely any more. I don't really expect anything from other people now. I just want to share. And it's not lonely, it's beautiful. I don't feel the need to rush around trying to please everyone either. I'm not here to fight other people's battles. I used to worry about that. I was a people-pleaser. But now all of that stuff no longer serves a purpose.

I'm comfortable in my own skin without needing the approval of others. I don't feel lonely because I know who I am and what I stand for. Enjoying my own company is enough. I have woken up to my place in life. I have glimpsed the broader picture. I don't even feel alone when I'm by myself any more.

It's part of what Mum said. I like the direction I'm taking my life now. And when I read what she wrote, I immediately caught the nuance because I'm finally engaged. It's about the direction I'm taking my life. It has nothing to do with where life is taking me. I see the light of responsibility very clearly now.

And I just want to share.

CHAPTER TWENTY

Waiting to Levitate

'Everything that life has to offer is right in front of your face'

You

Sunday

It's time to acknowledge something.

There is something that needs to be addressed. It's obvious this dialogue is not just a simple conversation with myself. It's become more than that. To be honest, I don't actually think it was ever just a simple conversation with myself.

And here I am again, trying to find a way to explain an x-factor. I find myself staring at another supposed contradiction.

But it is both somehow. From the very beginning of this thing, I have found comfort in knowing that no one else is reading this stuff. I write as if I'm the reader. I've held nothing back. There are several things that have helped keep me on track with this dialogue. And one of them is the fact that I haven't been concerned about anyone reading what I write.

It's been completely liberating. I would encourage anyone who wanted to listen, to take up something creative without worrying about pleasing anyone else. Just imagine what would happen if you took on a creative process without concern. Just start that thing you've always wanted to do, for no other reason, than to create.

That's what I've been doing. And it's felt amazing. From a nine-to-five perspective, it is the single greatest thing I have ever taken on. However on the odd occasion over the journey, I have wondered what I'm referring to when I use terms such as 'us' and 'we'. Coming from a place of simply writing to myself, I have questioned why I occasionally address a collective.

And now I'm happy to acknowledge something I have always known. This story will be for others. I find myself here so that others might as well. This dialogue is a sharing of something. It is fortified by the strength that comes with offering something up. From the beginning, I have been sharing my story. And I finally understand who I've been talking to. I know who this is for.

You.

Monday

If you are holding this book, I am talking to you.

I find myself writing these words so that you might find yourself reading them. And if you hear nothing else I have to say, hear what I'm about to. I am no better than you. We are no different from each other. I do not come to you in this story from high above anything. I am not here to show you the way to something.

And I have absolutely no intention of changing what I have to say or how I've been saying it. I'm not going to pivot away from the momentum of this story. We have come this far together because of a silent agreement. And I will not break that agreement by changing what's been going on.

Moving forward will be about sharing stuff.

I started writing because I wanted clarity. I wanted to change the things that kept going wrong for me. I particularly wanted to address the heartbreak of my life. I needed to know how to stop it from happening. But I never really considered how I was going to achieve that. I opened this conversation with myself because I knew it would help compartmentalise things. Initially, I didn't look past that. I thought that was the entire point of the process.

But now I see something much bigger. The fulfilment of your life is a sharing of something. The process of this story is a good example. And it's not just about what's being said here. It's more about the offering of something. There is a real strength to be found in sharing your life.

If you can't seem to find your way to something, then just offer it to someone else. If you feel somewhat lost about a thing, then share it with someone. And if you do that you might see this:

You can't share something you don't have.

Tuesday

One hundred and thirty three days, and the answer has been staring me in the face the whole time. Reaching your greatest potential is an act of creation. It's not something that is going to prove itself one day. It's not a type of validation that only a few people deserve. Your greatest potential is within you. And it's never been anywhere else. It's never been about earning something.

Achievements aren't going to get us there. And that's because there is nowhere to get. Everything we have ever needed to know is found within. Your highest reality is not going to reveal itself merely through hard work and achievements. Don't get me wrong, it's cool to reach a goal. But that's got nothing to do with what I'm talking about.

Everything that life has to offer is right in front of your face. It's always been those ding-dong moments that wake us up. It's never been about luck or winning something. Your greatest potential isn't a reward. It's got nothing to do with fairness or being a nice person. It's your birthright. It's a creation. It comes from the Creative Force of the Universe.

And if you can't get a handle on that, I'm going to ask you to do something. Please share it with someone.

And then see what happens. Everything you have ever wanted from the world is waiting for you. And if you can't see that, share what you want with someone. And know that it's impossible for you to do that, if you don't have it to begin with. Don't sit around waiting for what you want. Go out and share it. Then it'll be yours. You will have created it.

Ripples of Stillness

Wednesday

I want to slow down for a second. I don't want to get swept up in the stuff I've been writing recently. Everything is quite new and untouched. And it feels exciting. I'm seeing things I've never seen before. I'm looking at stuff I've been shying away from most of my life. But I don't want to move straight past the stuff that helped get me here.

Jess, Haylie and I went out to dinner tonight. It was great to slow everything down and spend time with them. That's no big newsflash though. They have always been enough. There's nothing to rant about beyond that. For a while there, my kids were the only reason I knew life could be amazing.

And I don't have much to say other than that. Except of course, that we saw an absolute genius on the way home from dinner. It's always the things you don't expect. It's the stuff you don't see coming.

We were half way home. We were behind a line of cars at a red light. There were a guy and a girl waiting at a bus stop right next to us. They looked like teenagers. They were wearing a mixture of gothic and hippie stuff. They seemed to be mucking around while they were waiting for the bus.

And then it happened. The smartest thing I have ever seen. The gothic-girl backed up five or six paces. She put her hands on her hips, looked to the sky and yelled something we couldn't hear. Then she ran in a straight line and attempted to fly. She stuck her left arm out, and launched into the air. It was genius. She was brilliant.

It's always the stuff you don't see coming. This young lady had worked it out. If you are going to try to fly, do it from a running start. If you want to test your potential with something so absurd, don't go jumping off stuff. You might hurt yourself. Plant your feet on the ground and try it from there. You're almost guaranteed not to break anything.

I'm telling you, the gothic-girl is a super hero.

You

Thursday

I have a friend who lives in Europe. He rocked up to my place today without warning. Marcus has lived away from Perth for over a decade. But he always comes home for Christmas. And we always catch up when he does.

We spent the entire day talking about each other's past year. I had a lot to tell him. It felt great to unpack what's been going on. Sometimes we need to hear stuff. The fact that Marcus didn't know anything about the past four or five months meant that I needed to explain things deliberately.

Marcus can handle anything. I think he could be the smartest guy I know. He's got a huge brain. And you can tell he relies on it. Talking about metaphysical stuff is not really his thing though. He finds it difficult not to be facetious when someone starts talking about spiritual things. But he kept that in check today. I think he saw that I was being sincere so he backed off.

That is, until he couldn't take it any more. Towards the end of our conversation, he asked what the point was. I didn't really understand the question. Marcus asked what the past few months had shown me. I took some time with the answer. I wasn't flippant with my response. I said that I understood now that we were not the struggles we face. We are not the things that stop us in life. I said I thought that anything was possible.

Marcus just looked at me and said: 'Oh really, then why don't you put your head through that table.' He pointed at my solid oak 30kg coffee table. I immediately thought about the girl yesterday. I remembered something critical to everything that's been going on.

That's what we do with our faith.

Friday

We take it to extremes. We push our faith to the limits. That was certainly true for me. When it came to living out my greatest potential, I was waiting to levitate. Having faith in myself was about the world proving something to me. I was waiting for God to pay me back for being a nice guy. I wanted the universe to notice.

I was no different to that flying gothic-girl. And I used to ask the same questions that Marcus asked yesterday. I have spent my life asking questions of doubt. And it's the very thing that has overshadowed my awareness of what the world has to offer. The questions were fuelled by doubt. And that was the very thing keeping me confused.

Having faith doesn't have to be about taking things to the extreme. If you need to prove something to yourself, then you're not being yourself in the first place. Expecting the world to prove something to you is not faith. It's a forgery of faith. And that sort of thing will only remove you from the responsibility of your life.

You have been given the chance to create the life you want. And you are doing it whether you want to or not. If you spend your time questioning things with doubt, then you will experience doubt. If you believe that the universe doesn't notice your good deeds, then you will go unnoticed.

You are constantly acting in accordance to your beliefs no matter what. And that's precisely what creates your experience. It is your faith that gets it done. You are a result of the life you see. You are the reflection of the things you give out to the world.

Pushing your beliefs to the extremes is about wanting more from life. It's about wishing for something. But at the deepest level, luck isn't going to prove anything to you. Everything that you are, comes from what you give out. Wishing for more is futile. Life will give you whatever you share. There is nothing out there that is more than you.

Saturday

I've never been able to find that genie in a bottle. As much as I've wished for luck, I've never found that magical thing. I guess the idea of luck has a place in this world. But sitting around waiting for it won't produce anything. All you get from the experience of waiting for something is the experience of waiting for something. If you spend your life sitting around doing nothing, then nothing will happen.

I can't help but think about the 'golden rule' again. Treat people the way you want to be treated. I see now that it's not really a rule. It's incomplete to say that it's an instruction. It's not something you should do if you want cool stuff to happen. It's a covenant. It is the universe telling you how things are.

You are always a reflection of how you treat others. Your relationships reflect how you treat yourself. If you feel like no one notices you, then get busy listening. If you desperately want to be heard, then find a way to be still. And pay attention to what you hear. You will have a hard time holding onto the belief that no one notices you, if you get busy noticing others.

When it comes to the things you have always wanted, you are the artist at the easel of life. Said more simply, you get what you give. It's not just a cliché. It's how the universe works. If your life is full of confusion, stop asking things of doubt. Approach your life with softness. It's the only way to change the hard times.

You are not the struggles you face. You are not the doubt that comes with that. You are the certainty that created those things. Such is the faith of a mustard seed.

Sunday

'Truly I tell you, if you have faith as small as a mustard seed, you can say to this mountain, 'move from here to there,' and it will move. Nothing will be impossible for you.'
Matthew 17:20

That message is found on the parchment paper of so many different religions throughout history. It's not just a Christian thing. In fact, it's not even about religion. What you believe about a thing will shape your life. That's an unstoppable force.

I've always assumed that having faith as small as a mustard seed was about trusting in something just a little bit. I thought it was about having just a smidgeon of the right kind of faith. I assumed that having a small amount of faith, in the right sort of thing, was all we needed. I thought the message was about hope.

But from a certain perspective, that line of thinking is incomplete. Faith doesn't have degrees of certainty. You cannot half believe something. What you believe is the central nervous system of your behaviour. And there are no degrees to that. There is a very simple way to describe having a small amount of faith.

Doubt.

If you say, 'sometimes I think I believe in something' you are describing an experience of doubt. And the thing that keeps that reality alive is you.

Don't get me wrong; you can approach your life with very little commitment. But that does not mean you question your beliefs. You can go through life without intent, but that doesn't imply that you have a small amount of faith.

What you believe is playing itself out no matter what. It is the conviction of certainty that makes it happen. You are that conviction. Having faith in your life is the substance and texture to everything that happens. You are the certainty of your beliefs. And if you wake up to that reality, nothing will be impossible for you.

Monday

Let's double back on something.

Gravity is good. Having faith in your life doesn't have to be taken to extremes. Waking up to the conviction of your beliefs has nothing to do with proving something to yourself. If you feel like you need to test the limits of your faith, then you believe in something very small. You are putting your faith in doubt. You are telling the universe you trust that.

Doubt is an essential thing. If you're patient, it will offer you clarity. But that doesn't mean you have to glorify the confusion in your life. The past five months have shown me that much at least. And I don't share that in order to show you something. I do it so that you might offer the same thing to someone else one day.

Waking up to your highest reality is not about standing out from the pack. It's about returning to it. The potential for your life has nothing to do with flying off into the sunset. We don't need to be trying to soar to great heights all the time. As my sister would say, just remain heavy on the earth. And she's right. If the apple couldn't fall from the tree, there would be no way for us to get home.

Your imagination is limitless. And that is no accident. But it doesn't always have to be about lofty and unrealistic stuff. There's a type of cliché that normally finds its way into this sort of story. It goes something like this:

'Nothing is impossible'

I love it. And it's fact. But it can't be tested. If you act unrealistically with that idea, then you will be unrealistic. On the other hand, if you remain heavy on the earth, anything will be possible. You will even be able to move things that normally seem too big to budge. You will be able to move emotional mountains. You can say to those things, move from here to there, and they will move.

And having done that, you will see the truth to your life.

CHAPTER TWENTY ONE

Echoes of Influence

'Who you are and what you do here shapes the experience of everyone you touch'

Tuesday

If I had the final say on what this book is about, it would be about how much I love Astrid. This is a story about love.

Everything I am doing here comes from how much she means to me. Losing her was the most heart-wrenching thing I have gone through. But in a weird way, I wouldn't change any of it. It's the catalyst to where I find myself now. It was the thing that woke me up. And all of this is because of how much I love her. I write to honour what Astrid and I shared.

I don't like thinking about the fact that she is leaving soon. I find it difficult to face. The whole situation reminds me that life isn't always easy. As much as it hurts to think about, I know it is something I have to deal with. It's an experience I need to have. And the reason I know that's true is because I'm currently feeling it. The hurt is necessary. If it weren't, it wouldn't be part of my experience.

The stuff that's meant to be is easy to recognise. All you have to do is look at what happened. But none of that means I'm happy about Astrid going. I mean, of course I'm devastated she's leaving. It feels like I'd give anything for her to stay. But then I realise that's not true. I wouldn't sacrifice everything to get her back. And it's pointless to pretend otherwise. That's called struggling. And it totally comes from within.

But as I write about it, I take a long deep breath. I guess we're about to become merely Facebook friends. I find that hard to comprehend. I'm a little concerned about how to tell Jess and Haylie. And so I haven't yet. Every time I've gone to explain it to them something has stopped me. I think it must be hope.

Wednesday

As much as the Astrid thing hurts, I know I am more than what it feels like. I won't push away what's happening. There's no point trying to run from it. I've just got to let the feeling download.

But that does not mean I have to become what I feel. I have thoughts of doubt and confusion about Astrid. But I also remember something critically important. And it is something that needs to be shared with as many people as possible. It is one of the central themes to this story. It was the beginning stages of everything that I have written over the past five months.

> *'Life is not what you think. You are more than what you think about. You are most certainly more than your doubts.'*

Thursday the 9th of August was when I started waking up. What took place back then is the reason I have been able to square off and be completely honest with myself. Detaching from the cycle of negativity I had created was a massive game-changer. It was like God put a microphone to my insights. I couldn't ignore them. They were so clear, I saw nothing else for a while.

The lines of this story are but an echo of influence to what took place then. It was the stillness in life that sharpened my awareness. I could see it everywhere. I stepped aside from all the negative stuff I was telling myself, and everything became so much brighter. From the stillness of the moment I saw a light of possibility everywhere I looked.

The potency of what happened has thinned over the past few months. The stuff we experience in life tends to fade over time. But this story has helped keep it alive. The experience might have thinned, but the influence of what took place has not. And none of it is about fairies and unicorns. The light in the stillness of your life is more grounded than that. It is entirely about choice.

Thursday

And yet the sadness took hold today.

It was the smallest thing that made it happen. I took Tristan to the airport. He is going away for Christmas and I wanted to see him before he left. I wanted to thank him for everything he has done for me lately. And I know he heard me loud and clear. It was great to send him off on such a positive note.

But as he was leaving to board the plane, something else occurred to me. I was waving goodbye, and I realised one of two things were about to happen. I am either going to be doing the same thing with Astrid soon, or I will continue to ignore her pending departure, and not get to see her leave at all. And each scenario completely sucks.

And then the sadness took over. After I left the airport I drove around aimlessly for about an hour. I was driving around in the same way I felt. Aimless. Thankfully I was aware that what I was going through was temporary. I knew it would eventually pass.

Without planning it, I ended up driving over to Bryce's place. But I couldn't get out of the car for some reason. I just sat there staring at his house. I was parked in his driveway for about 10 minutes before he came out. He walked around to the passenger side of my car and hopped in the front seat.

He didn't speak. We just sat in silence for a while. I started squeezing the steering wheel with my hands. Bryce said: 'So you're thinking about Astrid.' I nodded silently. And then I apologised for showing up in such a weird way. Bryce dismissed what I said with a wave of his hand.

We didn't really talk beyond that. We just sat quietly together. After a while Bryce opened the car door and said he was going back inside. He looked at me and spoke gently: 'Somewhere along the way you've found your voice. Maybe it's time to use it.'

RIPPLES *of* STILLNESS

Friday

There are going to be times in your life that suck. We are not here to only experience the good times. Sometimes things are going to get tough. You cannot control everything that happens in life. But you will always have choice. It's the mother of all paradoxes. It's this thing:

> *'The only thing you don't have a choice about is the fact that you always have a choice'*
> Simon Moxham

And if you can't see that, then look for it in others. Don't be afraid to share yourself. If you think you can't see something, but can recognise it in someone else, you will have changed your thought process. You can't recognise something in others unless you have it within yourself. The universe is a reflection of what you bring to it.

I went over to Mum's place today. It was the anticipation of what Bryce said yesterday that took me there. I woke this morning still feeling a bit restless about Astrid. So I went straight over to see Mum. And she didn't waste any time either. I didn't stay long.

As soon as we sat down, she asked if I knew the Hebrew meaning of my name. I said I didn't. She said the name Simon translates to 'he who listens and understands.' I went searching for the point. Mum asked another question: Did I know why she and Dad picked my name? Was I aware of the significance of the apostle Simon Peter?

Then she said something whilst looking away:

> *'And upon this rock I will build my church'*
> Matthew 16:18

She looked at me and asked if I knew what the passage meant. I said it was about faith. With a certain amount of tenacity, I said that I understood perfectly well what it meant. Mum replied gently: 'So you have listened and understood.'

I started getting really impatient. Mum walked straight to her front door and opened it. She looked at me and said: 'Now go and do something about it.'

And that's exactly why I decided to go after Astrid.

Saturday

I left Mum's place yesterday knowing exactly what I needed to do. And I had no idea how to do it.

But it seemed urgent. I should point out that Astrid and I have still been sending each other the odd email. We haven't done it much. And we haven't talked about anything too significant. I think we've both been trying to avoid talking about the elephant in the room. But I don't care about that stuff now.

It was time to reach out to her. And I didn't care that it could end badly. It wasn't about getting a result. It was about sharing how I feel about her. I don't really expect anything else. Astrid has a steely determination. When she makes up her mind about something, it's going to happen no matter what.

So I knew there wasn't really anything I could do to change her mind about leaving. But it didn't matter in the slightest. Throughout the past five months, I have been overly cautious not to bombard Astrid with too much emotional stuff. I wanted to give her the time and space she needed. I wanted everything about our friendship to be relaxed. And I have been very single-minded about that.

I forgot something pretty important. I forgot that beyond what I was doing, absolutely everything else was up for grabs. I remembered that the stillness of choice sat behind what I was telling myself. From wanting to give Astrid space, I forgot to share myself. I forgot about the vulnerability that comes with that.

I urgently wanted to talk to her. But she wasn't answering her phone. And then I remembered that she was still having regular contact with Nicola. I called her straight away. Nic explained that Astrid was working away again. I felt completely deflated. I didn't want to be patient today. I flippantly asked what I was meant to do next.

Nicola answered sharply: 'How is that even a question!'

My letter to Astrid

I come to you wanting absolutely nothing in return.
I am here to tell you what it feels like. I want you to know where I have been. It was from a place of darkness that we lost each other. I am sorry I turned my back on you over something so small.
I thought the struggles I faced were real. I assumed they were important. I hid behind the drama of my life so that no one could see me.
I was flippant with you.
I wanted your love to prove something to me. I unintentionally hurt you because I was blind to the pain I felt.
And so I write.
I am here to share something different with you now. I have come because you are worthy of more than I showed you.
This letter is my way of standing in front of you. I feel completely vulnerable. It feels like I should kneel before your beautiful life.
I see who you are because I know who I am now.
Ever since I lost you I have been looking for something.
Clarity.
I was not looking for a way back to you. I went looking for the truth to my life. And I found it when I stopped searching. I have seen a type of peace that poets write about.
And it's all because of what it feels like to love you.
The truth to life is about love. It's about softness and gentle things. And I have felt all of it. I finally love my place in this world. I don't stand in front of you now to talk you into anything. I am here to share myself with you.
And this is the how of it.
I would gladly give up everything I have come to know for you. Not to be a martyr or because I want to sacrifice something. But because I am awake now. And I want you to be part of it.
Everything I have come to know is but a silhouette of a shadow compared to what it feels like to love you.
This is my way of kneeling before your beautiful life.

Monday

Part of me thought it was about winning her back. But what I've been doing here was never about Astrid. It was about getting to know myself. It took being completely honest. Try to imagine what you would say if you were to have a conversation with your soul. Imagine what you would say if no one else was listening.

That's what I have been doing here. That's how this story came to be. After I emailed the letter to Astrid yesterday, I felt completely at peace with everything I have been doing. I don't know when she gets back from working away. And I still don't know the exact details of when she's going to Germany.

And none of it matters that much any more. Writing to Astrid was about sharing with her. It was about total vulnerability. Not in order to get something in return. But so that she might see who I am. It was about being generous for the sake of generosity. If you give in order to get something back, you are not really giving anything of worth.

Giving yourself to others isn't about getting results. It's about shaping the experience of life. Who you are, and what you do shapes the experience of everyone you touch. And the ripple effect never stops. That's because it's true for all of us.

Therefore, what you share with others spans everything. As you touch one, they touch another. And it never stops. It is always in motion. The sharing of you is always changing because it is moulded to the experience of everything. There would be no growth in the world if things never changed. There would be no experience of that without you. Who you are, and what you do with that helps shape the world. You are touching the lives of everyone you meet.

You are touching the face of God.

Tuesday

I woke this morning feeling completely at peace. Roughly seven hours of sleep, and yet it felt like I was awake through all of it. There is no one home but I know I'm not alone. I was lying in my bed staring at the ceiling again this morning. Everything was completely still. And it was from there, that I could feel the movement of life.

I started to think about my two beautiful daughters. They will be coming home today at lunchtime. I can't wait to see them. If I didn't know what it felt like to love them, I would have no place to start with everything else. And that is also true for the rest of my family. The reason I love my life so deeply is because of the people who are in it.

I thought about Tristan and Bryce. They have been so generous over the past few months. And it was a pleasure to return that to them. I thought about all of my other friends as well. I haven't mentioned too many other people in this story, but they still helped write these words.

I am not here in order to snag an amazing life for myself. It's not about grabbing something quickly. I am here to honour the people in my life. My fingers wrote this thing. But it was the influence of others that made it possible. And the gratitude I feel cannot be described quickly.

The influence of others wrote this story. And it's not limited to the people I've met. I'm also talking about the authors of the world. The sharing of this book comes from the sharing of others. I still have fleeting moments when I don't know how I will ever be able to thank everyone who helped me here. But then I realise something I've always known.

I just did.

CHAPTER TWENTY TWO

The Most Extraordinary Thing

'You are the fulfilment of love'

You

Wednesday

The girls and I decided to go on a picnic today. It was a beautiful day so we decided to take our puppy to the South Perth foreshore. December rocks in our family. There are birthdays all over the place. Christmas rules. And New Year's Eve always caps everything off nicely.

I was buzzing this morning. I spent most of it preparing food for the picnic. I never knew doing household chores could feel so exciting. Not so much with the stillness for me today. I was pinging. I loved it. But I was forced to slow down a little when I thought it was time to go. I had packed the car. I called out to the girls about leaving. But Jess came out of her room and said that she invited Sophie (one of her school friends) to come with us. So we had to wait.

I got back to doing chores and stuff. I was elbow deep in soapsuds when Sophie rang the doorbell. I called out to Jess. After a few seconds Sophie knocked on the door. I impatiently yelled for someone to let her in. But nothing happened. I splashed the dishwater off my hands and stomped to the front door. Jess and Haylie were standing in the entry to our house looking at me. I said abruptly: 'Open the bloody door for God's sake!' And then I flung it open.

Astrid was standing in front of me. And she was holding the teddy bear with the red bowtie.

I froze.

She had a tear in her eye. Her hands were shaking a little. Her shoulders dipped ever so slightly. I saw her eyes ask me something before she spoke. She said: 'For me.'

I whispered without thinking:

'Yes.'

She replied: 'We'll stay if you will.'

I don't know why, but I turned to Jess and Haylie and said: 'But what about the girls, I haven't…' I saw Haylie trying to conceal her joy by covering her mouth. Jess was smiling with tears in her eyes. They already knew. Haylie explained that Astrid spoke to them two nights ago. I immediately sat down in front of her. It was all I could do.

Astrid crouched down. She touched her forehead on mine.

I said: 'Have you come back to me?'

Jess and Haylie hugged both of us. Astrid touched the side of my face gently and said: 'You found me again.'

YOU

Thursday

Perhaps I am about to say the most shocking thing of all.

I've almost run out of words. There's not much more to say. And people who know me will tell you that never happens. I'm not trying to end this abruptly. It just feels like I've said enough. And to be honest, I thought that before yesterday. My purpose here has been slowly wrapping up for a while now.

I opened my laptop this morning prepared to explain the joy I feel about Astrid coming back to us. I wanted to talk about it all day. I was as happy today, as when my two beautiful daughters came into the world. And I was fully prepared to share that. I went to write, but my fingers wouldn't move. I waited, and nothing happened.

I decided to come back here later. I tried to write after lunch but I got nothing again. As I sit here writing now, it's 11:37pm. Jess and Haylie are sleeping. The house is completely quiet. I went to bed an hour ago, but I couldn't get to sleep. I was thinking about Astrid. The love I feel for her was keeping me awake. I can't wait to build a new life with her.

Part of me wondered if yesterday signified the end to this. I was lying in bed an hour ago wondering if I'm done. And then I realised something. This dialogue has never really been exclusively about Astrid and me. I've been sharing about us. But that doesn't mean this story has to end because of what happened yesterday. This thing wasn't written just for that. It was written for you.

I am here tonight for exactly the same reason I started writing five months ago. I am here to be with you. This story was never just about me. It has always been about us. And I want to be with you for just a little bit longer.

Friday

There is something about this experience that I have not shared with you yet. It's not significant. And I'm sure you have already sensed it anyway. In fact, you probably picked up on it well before I did. I realised this morning that this story has been somewhat of a nocturnal one. As I've said previously, I have no set routine about when I write. There are no rules I follow before I come here. But having said that, most of what I've had to say has been said late at night.

But none of that means I have spent my days waiting. It's not like I sat around waiting for inspiration. What we have shared together has nothing to do with stuff happening to us. We haven't come this far because of luck. We have created our experience of this story together.

And when it comes to living the sort of life you want, I say this to you. Try not to waste too much energy waiting for things. Don't spend too much time waiting for the world to prove something to you. I'm not suggesting you should overcrowd your life with busyness. Sometimes being busy can get quite addictive. And if we allow ourselves to get swept up by that stuff, we might find ourselves wanting to hide there.

There are times in life when we need to relax. There's nothing wrong with chilling out on the couch. But my experience tells me that if you do that sort of thing too much, you could miss out on something pretty important - everything else.

You are a reflection of the life you see. If you spend your life waiting, it will be returned to you. The people in your life will wait with you as long as they can. The stuff you've always dreamed about will do the same. Your greatest potential awaits you. And it is infinitely more patient than anyone of us could ever be. Instead of wasting your energy testing all that stuff, try meeting it on common ground.

Saturday

Since the moment I started writing, I have been talking about fulfilment. I opened this dialogue because I thought it was missing. I started writing because it felt like I had none. And even though I wasn't aware of it, I went looking for the fulfilment of my life with the words that we are sharing together right now.

I have always felt throughout my life that happiness was fleeting. And the more I've looked into it, the more I want to be gentle. It's not because I think happiness is fragile. And it's not because I want to preserve it for as long as possible. I am not suggesting that happiness is like a thirsty flower that needs too much work.

I want to be gentle with my happiness because I have remembered something about it that never ends. I have finally seen the thing that has always been staring me right in the face. And on the surface, it doesn't even seem all that romantic. But if you look deeply, you will see the truth to your life.

It's this thing:

If happiness didn't come and go, you would not be able to experience anything else. If life was not always on the move, we would not be self-aware. Experience is not just about one thing. We have not come for the fulfilment of just one thing. We are the experience of life. We come here after a cosmos of conversations.

From the moment I started to share this story, I have been looking for the fulfilment of my life. In some way, on some level, I guess we find ourselves here together for the same reasons. I've kept up with this thing for the same reason you've probably kept reading it. We have been looking for the fulfilment of something. But throughout these chapters, I've remembered perhaps the most important thing of all.

There is no distance between you and the love in the world. You don't have to look for it. It's within you. Don't try reaching for it. You are already the fulfilment of love. Share. Just share it with others.

That's all.

Sunday

I actually feel a little nervous.

But at the same time, I feel so awake. I feel completely at peace. The anticipation of what's going to happen next leaves me a little nervous. Not because I'm afraid of the unknown. But because I am finally at a place in my life where I want to embrace every part of it. And it fills me with nervous excitement.

I look out of my kitchen window, and I'm staring into the face of possibility again. I feel the stillness of life in every fibre of my being. I finally have no questions to ask of the world. I can see a light of possibility everywhere. It's huge. It's still. It's choice. And I stand before it now.

We are not finishing up because I want to rush off and hang out with Astrid. From the beginning of this story, I have been using my insights to explore the silence of my inner world. And you have been reading these words to explore yours. But I have no more questions to ask.

There is something I want to give you though. It's the greatest gift I have to offer. And for now, I'll have to give it to you here. It's the only way I can get it to you. We've come to the end of this thing together so that I can say this to you...

Thank you.

You have brought this story to life. And it takes my breath away.

Remember, you are so amazing. Please share yourself. Please give that gift to others. You are worthy of all of it. You can create anything. Your life is so amazing. There's no one else like you. And the most extraordinary thing about all of that is this:

You've known that your entire life.

You

Monday *(On the eve of the New Year)*

This is how we find out what happens next.